WRITTEN
OUT OF
HISTORY

WRITTEN OUT OF HISTORY

The Forgotten Founders
Who Fought Big Government

SENATOR
MIKE LEE

SENTINEL

Sentinel
An imprint of Penguin Random House LLC
375 Hudson Street
New York, New York 10014
penguin.com

Most Sentinel books are available at a discount when purchased in quantity for sales promotions or corporate use. Special editions, which include personalized covers, excerpts, and corporate imprints, can be created when purchased in large quantities. For more information, please call (212) 572-2232 or e-mail specialmarkets@penguinrandomhouse.com. Your local bookstore can also assist with discounted bulk purchases using the Penguin Random House corporate Business-to-Business program. For assistance in locating a participating retailer, e-mail B2B@penguinrandomhouse.com.

ISBN 9780399564451 (hardcover)
ISBN 9780399564475 (e-book)

Printed in the United States of America
10 9 8 7 6 5

To my parents, Rex and Janet Lee

CONTENTS

CONTENTS

INTRODUCTION
The Hamilton Effect

Washington. Adams. Jefferson. Madison.

These are the names of the first four presidents of the United States of America, but they are also the names of the men who were among the most prominent voices of our founding era. There are other founders, indeed, who, though they never attained our nation's highest office, still live on in our history—Benjamin Franklin, John Hancock, and, most notably, Alexander Hamilton among them.

However, other founders, as relevant but with names not as well known, are missing from our nation's popular history. Some individuals whose words and ideas contributed much to the founding of the nation have been relegated to the footnotes of history. And even others have, as a practical matter, been expunged from history altogether. The familiar narrative many of us were taught as children about our founding—that great men came together to forge a constitution that set America on its present course—isn't exactly true, either. At least it isn't complete.

Most Americans can name only a few of the nearly sixty men who were sent to the 1787 convention that produced our Constitution; fewer still know about the sixteen attendees who, for various reasons, never signed the document, including the three who defiantly refused. A number of those who attended the convention even actively campaigned against its final product. Many men who had given everything they had for independence—pledging their lives, fortunes, and sacred honor to resist a distant, remote government that recognized no limitations on its sovereign power—believed the Constitution would lead to the new nation's ruin. And the delegates who did sign the Constitution, and fought vigorously for its adoption, had no intention of creating a sprawling, unaccountable federal bureaucracy like the one we have in Washington, DC, today. Why don't we know more about these delegates?

There were others who, while not delegates, still had a profound effect on the development of the American Republic. There were women, Native Americans, and African Americans who played a significant role in the fight for independence and in the thinking that went into our Constitution. Why are those names absent from popular history?

To find the answers to these questions, we must take a journey back to the early days of our Republic.

* * *

During the debates surrounding the Constitution's drafting and ratification, the doubts, skepticism, and outright fear of what the Constitution would bring ultimately made the document stronger and more just. That may sound strange to us in the twenty-first century, but remember: the founders, by declaring their independence from Great Britain and building their own system from scratch, had placed themselves in uncharted territory. The men—each in his own right, sometimes working together and often not—were unusually gifted, but they were still making this up as they went along. What became our governing document was the result of a brilliant compromise between the Anti-Federalists and the Federalists—between those who championed a divided and limited but strong central government, and those who feared that almost any central government would expand its authority at the expense of individual liberty and state autonomy.

We today are the beneficiaries of that Great Compromise, but too many of us don't fully understand it. And that is because history, over time, has tended to remember *only one side* of the argument, crowding out dissenting voices and obscuring the full story of the American experiment. In the last century, in particular, historians and politicians who consider themselves more enlightened than the founders—and believe in the power of bureaucrats to manage the affairs of an entire country from a distant capital—have done special damage to the legacy of the founding generation, a legacy that warned against the dangers of a distant, centralized government.

Most of us, for example, are never presented with the arguments raised by the Anti-Federalists, who opposed the Constitution's ratification based on concerns that it would vest too much power in the federal government and thereby imperil liberty. And just as disturbing, many of the Federalists have been mischaracterized as early advocates of big government. Some have tried to portray the founders as proto-progressives, even though the founders lived a full century before there was anything even resembling a "progressive." Those perpetuating this mischaracterization have done so by erasing the truth that nearly every founder shared a healthy skepticism of a large federal bureaucracy—one that might eventually mimic some of the worst features of the very government they had just fought a revolution to escape.

No one living in America in the late eighteenth century—certainly none of the brilliant minds who forged our founding documents—could have contemplated just how strong, or how large, that government would become. Nor could they have imagined how much control the city named for George Washington would come to have over ordinary citizens.

Take Alexander Hamilton, for example, a brilliant man who spoke up during the debates over the Constitution as one of the most fervent advocates of a stronger national government. In 2016 Hillary Clinton's presidential campaign adopted Hamilton as something of a mascot—quoting the eponymous hit show written by Lin-Manuel Miranda in speeches and renting out the entirety of Broadway's Richard Rodgers Theatre, where the musical was performed for a fundraiser. A century earlier, Herbert Croly, one of the most influential progressive intellectuals of the period and cofounder of *The New Republic*, praised Hamilton for advocating a policy of "active interference with the natural course of American economic and political business and its regulation and guidance in the national direction."[1]

Many on the left who are staunch advocates of big government have expressed a kinship with Alexander Hamilton—but theirs is a perverted vision. It is true that Hamilton fought vigorously for ratification of the Constitution. It is true that he believed that a federal government should have the power to accomplish a number of things that it could not do under the Articles of Confederation. But what Hamilton's fans on the left neglect to mention, or in some cases don't even realize, is that Alexander Hamilton never envisioned—and certainly never favored—the sort of massive, intrusive, unaccountable federal government that today thrives in Washington, DC. More to the point, once the Constitution was in place, he scoffed at and ridiculed the idea that the federal government could be anything other than the modest, divided, and tightly constrained government outlined in that document.

In *The Federalist Papers*, a series of documents published throughout the colonies in support of the new Constitution, Hamilton responded to concerns articulated by many of our founders—including people you will meet in this book—that the Constitution could become a Trojan horse for oppressive government. Hamilton thought such a notion ludicrous, even paranoid. "Allowing the utmost latitude to the love of power which any reasonable man can require"—he wrote in *Federalist* number 17 under the name "Publius"—"I confess I am at a loss to discover what temptation the persons intrusted with the administration of the general government could ever feel to divest the States of the authorities of that description." The "government of the Union" could never become "too powerful . . . to enable it to absorb those residuary authorities, which it might be judged proper to leave with the States for local purposes . . . it is therefore improbable that there should exist a disposition in the federal councils to usurp the powers with which they are connected; because the attempt to exercise those powers would be as troublesome as it would be nugatory [insignificant]; and the possession of them, for that reason, would contribute nothing to the dignity, to the importance, or to the splendor of the national government."[2]

Supposing that such a perversion of the Constitution was attempted, Hamilton wrote, the states and localities would always be more powerful than a central government. "It will always be far more easy for the State governments to encroach upon the national authorities than for the national government to encroach upon the State authorities," he said.[3] In *Federalist* number 32, Hamilton explained that "State governments would clearly retain all the rights of sovereignty which they before had" prior to the Constitution's enactment, as long as those powers had not been "exclusively delegated" to the federal government—making the Constitution's real goal, in Hamilton's view "only . . . a partial union or consolidation."[4]

This was also a view shared by his colleague, and fellow advocate for the Constitution, James Madison, who wrote in *Federalist* number 45 that "the powers delegated by the proposed Constitution to the federal government are few and defined. Those which are to remain in the State governments are numerous and indefinite."[5]

In short, their view of what the federal government—first in Philadelphia and then in Washington, DC—was meant to be, and what the Constitution clearly intended, is not at all what that government has become over the last eighty years. They did not envision a Congress that would take more and more power from states and localities, regulating nearly every aspect of human existence— education, agriculture, health care, commerce, transportation, among others. They did not envision a Supreme Court that would find thin justifications in the Constitution to support such a massive federal expansion. They did not envision a Congress so weak and willing to delegate its lawmaking power to unaccountable bureaucrats in the executive branch and judges in the judicial branch.

Even Alexander Hamilton, the most forceful advocate for a strong and active national government, believed deeply in checks and balances that would strictly limit the government's power.

None of this, by the way, is the fault of the Constitution, which was and remains a masterpiece, the greatest governing document ever devised by human beings. This happened because we've lost any sense of what federal power the founders intended the Constitution to allow, and what it intended to limit. We've lost to history some of the most prescient warnings offered by our founders— especially those most fiercely resistant to the Constitution and skeptical of big government—because we've never been allowed to hear them in the first place.

Progressive, big-government advocates like to politicize their history. They twist history to suit their ends. They ignore and ultimately erase history when it stands in their way. They always seek more power, and part of that means changing the historical narrative to confer legitimacy. Call it the "Hamilton Effect." But if we knew our history—the true and complete stories of how our nation came to be—we'd know how to fight back against the progressive agenda. We'd be a lot less likely to accept their overreach.

That's why I've written this book. In my previous book, *Our Lost Constitution: The Willful Subversion of America's Founding Document,* I demonstrated how various provisions of the Constitution had been deliberately distorted far beyond the founders' intentions in order to increase power in Washington, DC. Indeed, in many, many cases that power has been diverted from the people's representatives in Congress to unelected bureaucrats in a multitude of agencies and departments in the executive branch. To their credit, there were founders who warned us of this outcome. Why then is it that those who did so most presciently, vocally, and aggressively have been erased from our collective history? This presents something of a paradox: the more accurately a founder predicted the excessive accumulation of power under the Constitution, the less likely we are to celebrate (or even to mention) them in our history books.

This book seeks to remedy this imbalance—by highlighting the stories not only of those who helped to make the Constitution possible, but also of those who warned about its misapplication and misinterpretation. Their stories are important, especially today, because the battle in which these men and women were engaged more than two centuries ago is still being waged. Within these pages is a true, alternative history of our nation's founding, populated with varied characters who foretold with great accuracy the dangers of a powerful federal government—one that I see every day in Washington's halls of power. The process of rediscovering who these people were, what they did, what they fought for, and why they did so is one of the best ways of recovering the lost (but valuable) principles of limited government.

It is time to reintroduce to the American people the founders whose stories have been lost.

As we rediscover those stories and internalize the lessons they can teach us—making them once again part of our national historical and political conversation—we will become better equipped to restore key constitutional protections. Those protections are there for good reasons (many of which are discussed in this book) and, once restored, will bless the lives of all Americans.

Throughout this book, you will meet a number of Americans who are not household names but who should be. Some warned against the dangers of big government generally, while others fought to protect specific individual liberties. Let us introduce them here:

- Aaron Burr, an early victim of big government, whose "trial of the century" in the early 1800s against President Thomas Jefferson defined the limits of executive power and warned of its potential for abuse;
- Luther Martin, who refused to sign the Constitution based on what he perceived as its failure to protect individual rights;
- Mercy Otis Warren, one of America's first female writers and a John Adams protégée, who spent her life warning against the encroachment of federal power;
- Canasatego, an Iroquois chief, who taught Benjamin Franklin the basic principles behind the separation of powers and confederate government;
- Elbridge Gerry, who argued strongly for what would become the Bill of Rights;
- Mum Bett, a slave in Massachusetts, who saw her country struggle for freedom and was inspired to seek her own in a landmark case in which she argued that certain natural rights superseded unjust laws;

- James Otis, whose fight against the British Crown led to the development of search-and-seizure laws, protecting private property from government intrusion; and
- George Mason, the founder who fought and warned against government intrusion into commerce between individuals and states.

How much do we know about any of these leaders? Most of us tragically know too little. Some of this knowledge deficit could certainly be attributed to benign neglect; for one reason or another, some stories that should be remembered nonetheless fade from a society's historical understanding. At least some of it, however, likely stems from the well-understood fact that history is written by the winners. And in today's America, those who are winning are champions of big government. Consequently, if you don't fit a certain vision of history—if your story is inconvenient to the notion that we all benefit from a strong central government in which every aspect of human existence can be regulated by bureaucratic experts in Washington—then you run the risk of being written out of history.

WRITTEN
OUT OF
HISTORY

CHAPTER 1

Aaron Burr and the Abuse of Executive Power

Treason against the United States, shall consist only in levying War against them, or in adhering to their Enemies, giving them Aid and Comfort. No person shall be convicted of Treason unless on the Testimony of two Witnesses to the same overt Act, or on Confession in open Court.

The Congress shall have Power to declare the Punishment of Treason, but no Attainder of Treason shall work Corruption of Blood, or Forfeiture except during the Life of the Person attainted.

—U.S. Constitution, Article III, Section 3

For some twenty days, he had traveled in a carriage over mud-lined roads and rocky trails. "The captive," as he was described, "wore the same clothing in which he had been arrested: a floppy, dirty-white hat, and an old blanket coat that a river man might put on to keep warm," but his boots were still so shiny that they caught the eye.[1]

Surrounded by serious men, armed and mounted on horseback, the carriage's occupant finally could take a breath of fresh air when he arrived in Richmond, Virginia, on March 26, 1807. A few hundred miles south of the Executive Mansion he had once hoped to occupy, he was due to meet his destiny.[2] This prisoner was no ordinary villain; indeed, he was one of America's more prominent Founding Fathers: a Revolutionary War hero and a servant of the early Republic, the former governor of New York, the former vice president of the United States, a man who came within a few votes of the presidency itself. Aaron Burr was now under arrest.

This scene would have been impossible to imagine just a few short years ago, back when Burr's political star was on the rise. The son of the president of Princeton University, he initially studied law under Tapping Reeve, who was married to Burr's sister, Sarah ("Sally"), and would go on to serve as one of Mum Bett's attorneys in her famous fight to win her freedom. But young Aaron abandoned academic pursuits to enlist in the Continental Army in 1775. He had suffered with the rest of Washington's troops at Valley Forge. He went on to represent his native New York in the United States Senate and later in the New York legislature, eventually becoming vice president of the United States. Now he was in federal custody on the orders of his onetime colleague and rival, the president of the United States himself—Thomas Jefferson.

Among our Founding Fathers, Thomas Jefferson certainly stands out as one of the most revered. The Man from Monticello was the author of the Declaration of Independence, a fervent advocate for the American Republic, the founder of the University of Virginia, and the ingenious visionary who nearly doubled the size of our then nation with the Louisiana Purchase. But Thomas Jefferson had his excesses, too—and his moral failings. He was, of course, like many founders, a slaveholder. And as a politician and chief executive he demonstrated a capacity for deception and even corruption. There was no greater example of this failing than in his long-standing personal and political vendetta against his rival, Aaron Burr—a man who served as Jefferson's vice president and whom Jefferson single-handedly tried to convict of treason, a capital offense.

Our nation was still young. The Constitution under which the United States was governed had been enacted just twenty years earlier. The people had elected only their third president. Yet the temptation for executive overreach was already rearing its head. Thomas Jefferson pushed the boundaries of responsible executive power in a quest to bring down Aaron Burr in a court of law once and for all. Even before the trial began, Jefferson would expend relentless efforts to convict Burr in the court of public opinion, but the former vice president was determined to mount a defense. And he possessed some advantages in that effort. In fact, Burr was a far more complicated figure than many of his contemporaries—or history—would ever acknowledge. Aaron Burr's fatal mistake was running afoul of the leaders of his time, and because of that, he has been relegated to history as merely a traitor. His full story was twisted, and his truth was written out of history.

"I'd Rather Not Live Than Not Be the Daughter of Such a Man"

Part of the secret to Aaron Burr's early political success lay in his social success. And the secret behind *that* was his daughter, Theodosia. She was a consummate hostess at her family's New York mansion, greeting her guests warmly, as she always did, with a charming smile and reassuring words.

By 1791 Theodosia Burr was only fourteen years old, but she already carried herself with an erudition and confidence that belied her youth. The dark-haired young woman was Aaron Burr's eldest child and, after her mother's death three years earlier, had become the hostess of Richmond Hill, the elegant Burr manse in what would eventually evolve into Manhattan's Greenwich Village. This had grown to be a central hub of the New York social scene—and a not-so-secret base for plotting Aaron Burr's considerable political aspirations, of which Theodosia was a willing and worthy conspirator.

Her father, nearing the end of his tenure as New York's attorney general, had doted on the girl from an early age. It was at Burr's insistence and under his close direction that Theodosia was trained in mathematics, classics, language, and music—a great departure from most women of the day. Burr's home boasted a library filled with books that he introduced to his daughter as soon as she was able to read, engendering in the child an early and sincere love of literature.

Theodosia was to be no idle hostess. Occupation, Burr had long lectured his daughter, was essential to maintaining command over one's self.[3] Whenever he was away, he left detailed instructions to her tutors and resolved to fire any who did not prove up to Burr's high expectations. As a result, Theodosia became one of the best-educated women in America, acclaimed for her knowledge and accomplishment—skills she also lent in service to her kind and beloved father. "I'd rather not live," she once contended, "than not be the daughter of such a man."[4]

It was on behalf of Aaron Burr's political interests that Theodosia would turn Richmond Hill, set high on a hill overlooking the New Jersey shoreline, into *the* gathering spot in New York City—attracting visitors who ranged from Joseph Brant, the chief of the Six Nations of the Iroquois, to Alexander Hamilton (she counted his wife and children among her friends) and the acclaimed Virginian, Thomas Jefferson, who shared her father's skepticism of the Federalist Party and its attempts to amass power in the central government.

Her father would entertain there, as one chronicler later put it, "with a lavishness that eventually bankrupted him."[5] He was never a man to control his impulses, which more than one enemy believed would someday be his undoing. But at this point, that was a matter far beyond young Theodosia's understanding or concern. What she knew for certain was that her father was destined for great things— and she would do everything in her power to help him achieve them.

In the end, it was not Burr's lavish entertainment that caused his downfall, as some had predicted. But following his impulses did get him into trouble.

Altering the Deal

As the cold February winds howled outside, Thomas Jefferson paced in the study of his mountaintop estate at Monticello. The year 1801 was already more than a month in, and the contentious election of 1800 was still to be decided. But Jefferson did not like the way things looked in the middle of this long, cold winter. Aaron Burr stood a good chance of being elected president of the United States—but only after double-crossing his supposed political ally—Jefferson himself.

It had been an ugly election. Jefferson had been called a coward, accused of hunkering down at Monticello while others fought in the Revolution. Adams, in turn, had been attacked as a monarchist, as senile, and even—in the words of Alexander Hamilton—as a man with an "ungovernable temper."[6] Jefferson had savaged Adams, his former colleague and the sitting chief executive, for presiding over an administration that he believed ushered in a "reign of witches"— concentrating the country's worst fears about a powerful central government corrupted by Wall Street merchant and banking interests under the Federalist Party.[7] An unapologetic Francophile, Jefferson believed Adams's obvious affinity for England hinted at a return to British-style monarchy. "I have sworn upon the altar of God eternal hostility against every form of tyranny over the mind of Man," Jefferson wrote.[8] As for Aaron Burr, he was widely reviled as power hungry, and as a man who was devoid of any core beliefs, but willing to espouse any that would aid in his ascent. In reality, while Burr was by and large an Anti-Federalist Republican, his true passion was politics for the sport of it, which made him a formidable campaigner.

Most observers concluded early in the race that Jefferson had the presidency locked up against the hapless Adams, whose administration was embroiled in crises foreign and domestic—including a vicious struggle between France and England for America's allegiance. And Jefferson's own qualifications for the office were impressive, considering his distinguished career as a legislator, wartime governor, member of Congress, foreign minister, and secretary of state.

He had sought the office before. After George Washington declined to seek a third term as president, Jefferson was a leading candidate in the race to replace him. But in the election of 1796, Jefferson ultimately finished second to John Adams by a slim margin of 71 electoral votes to 68, making him Adams's vice president (pursuant to provisions of the Constitution in effect at that time).

Now it looked as though Jefferson was going to be robbed— once again—of the victory he felt he so deserved. The electoral vote in the November 1800 election had deadlocked—73 votes for Thomas Jefferson, 73 for Burr, 65 for the incumbent John Adams, and 64 for South Carolina's Charles Pinckney. Both Jefferson and Burr had run under the Democratic-Republican Party banner, though Jefferson had clearly been the party's preference. A finish behind Burr— forcing Jefferson again into the vice presidency, and again under a man he distrusted—would be an unmitigated, humiliating defeat.

Still, the Virginian had tried to make a deal with the New Yorker. A few months earlier, in December, with the election's outcome still uncertain, Jefferson had written to Burr a cryptic note that seemed to imply that he would give Burr, as vice president, more power than was customary. In response, Burr pledged to "disclaim all competition" with Jefferson and looked forward to serving his administration.[9]

Even assuming that Burr had ever meant those words, they came with an expiration date. By February, with an unprecedented electoral deadlock, Burr was actively campaigning for the presidency. He had even managed to reach an alliance with many in the Federalist Party who despised Jefferson, and who were in a position to throw the election to Burr if the contest was decided in the House of Representatives.[10]

Having learned of Burr's plans, Jefferson warned John Adams that any attempt "to defeat the Presidential election" with the assistance of Adams's fellow Federalists in Congress would "produce resistance by force, and incalculable consequences."[11] In the shadow of the French Revolution—which had thrown France into bloody and violent chaos, and of which Jefferson had become an ardent champion—the Virginian's comment could not be dismissed as an idle threat.

Ultimately it would be Federalists like Alexander Hamilton— who found Burr "without scruple" and "unprincipled"—who would turn the tide in Jefferson's direction. There were even rumors that Jefferson had cut his own secret deal with certain Federalists. But no holds were barred; Burr simply had to be stopped. To Jefferson, Burr had proved himself a man who was duplicitous—a double-dealer with an ambition that knew no bounds. (More than a few harbored this view of Jefferson as well.) Regardless, Burr's "betrayal" of Jefferson would not be forgotten. Burr's electoral votes might let him become vice president—there was little Jefferson could do to stop that—but Jefferson would never bring Burr into his confidence or esteem. Not ever.

Ambition Turns Deadly

Aaron Burr watched the man's body fall to the ground, twisting and wrenching in agony. The ball fired from Burr's pistol had inflicted a mortal wound. The next day—June 12, 1804—Burr's victim, Alexander Hamilton, would take his last breath.

Officially, the vice president's duel with Hamilton was illegal in their home state of New York, which is why they had traveled to Weehawken, New Jersey, for the confrontation. (New Jersey also prohibited dueling but was less likely than New York to enforce the ban.)

The confrontation had been years in the making—the result of two bright, ambitious men vying for power and prominence in the cutthroat world of New York politics. After seeking—and losing—the New York governorship, Burr took issue with a "despicable opinion" Hamilton had expressed against him at a dinner party.[12] At the dawn of the nineteenth century, insults aimed at men of prominence were not taken lightly and often resulted in confrontation. To put it mildly, this was no less true when the person being insulted was the sitting vice president of the United States. Burr concluded that he had endured enough already—Jefferson-sympathetic newspapers had gone after Burr's reputation almost from his first day in office, three years earlier.[13] And the latest slur out of Hamilton's mouth was only the most recent in a long list of the former Treasury secretary's vicious broadsides against Burr. In fact, it paled in comparison to some of Hamilton's earlier charges: that Burr's "very friends do not insist on his integrity";[14] that "he will court and employ able and daring scoundrels";[15] that "his conduct indicates [he seeks] Supreme power in his own person."[16]

Finally fed up, Burr issued his challenge. While questions remain as to Hamilton's intentions, Burr at least contemplated a fatal outcome. The night before the duel, he wrote a letter to the one living person who really mattered to him: "I am indebted to you, my dearest Theodosia, for a very great portion of the happiness I have enjoyed in this life."[17]

The encounter at Weehawken the next day would forever define Burr's role in history. Hamilton's death led to a public outcry and further cemented Burr's public reputation as a scoundrel.[18] The sitting vice president was charged with murder in New Jersey and New York, though neither case made it to trial. Burr returned to Washington to finish his term as vice president, where he was conspicuously ignored by Jefferson. Until, of course, he proved useful.

Burr Checks Presidential Power

Poor, frail, and doddering, Judge John Pickering had been the first victim of the Jeffersonian-dominated Congress. Jefferson's lieutenants in the Senate—members of the president's recently formed Democratic-Republican Party—had begun targeting Federalist judges for removal from the bench, and Pickering, whose own defense counsel labeled him insane, offered an easy scalp.[19] But on the day that Pickering's trial in the Senate ended with a party-line vote to convict, the House of Representatives formally impeached Jefferson's next intended victim. And this one was more formidable—Supreme Court Justice Samuel Chase, who had been appointed to the High Court by none other than George Washington.

For all of his election-year taunting of John Adams as a would-be monarch, Jefferson himself certainly seemed eager to rule by presidential fiat. He was especially ruthless when targeting his political enemies for impeachment. Justice Chase had been an outspoken opponent of the Jefferson administration, warning (correctly) that the president sought removal of all critical federal judges on various pretexts in order to install "timid and compliant judges" in their places.[20] Others warned that the impeachment trial of Chase was "the entering wedge to the complete annihilation of our wise and independent judiciary."[21] Jefferson himself had directed a member of the Senate to file impeachment charges against Chase. But the pièce de résistance was that President Jefferson was personally overseeing the proceedings.[22]

Since its opening on January 2, 1805, the impeachment trial of Chase had been riveting the capital. It also placed the focus squarely on the probity not only of the Jeffersonian-dominated Senate but also of the officer presiding over the trial—Vice President Aaron Burr.

Burr was a "lame duck" vice president, having been dropped from Jefferson's re-election ticket in the 1804 election. The Hamilton duel had been the final straw that prompted the Democratic-Republicans to seek to remove Burr, and Jefferson was not sorry to see him go.

But in the days leading up to the Chase trial, during which Jefferson knew that Burr would play a key role, the president's tone changed. Jefferson began to court Burr like a long-lost friend, literally and figuratively bringing him in from the cold. Burr had been invited to dine in the President's House. Jefferson had even asked him to suggest nominees to fill important positions in the new Louisiana Territory (recently purchased for a pittance from France), and appointed three of his vice president's favored candidates, among them Burr's stepson and his brother-in-law.[23]

But if Jefferson thought Burr was going to play ball with him, he would be disappointed. Burr had found his calling in the Senate and revered the institution, which he once proclaimed "a citadel of law, of order, of liberty." "It is here, in this exalted refuge," Burr said of the upper chamber, where robust, sincere debate could occur. "[H]ere, if anywhere, will resistance be made to the storms of political frenzy and the silent arts of corruption; and if the Constitution be destined ever to perish by the sacrilegious hands of the demagogue or the usurper, which God avert, its expiring agonies will be witnessed on this floor."[24] As vice president and presiding officer of the Senate—the vice president's constitutional role—Burr won surprising acclaim from across the political spectrum for his respect for the august body's traditions and constitutional functions.

Burr also earned praise for his "judicial manner" in presiding over the Chase impeachment trial. He studiously resisted any effort to enforce Jefferson's will on the outcome. His presence was felt in touches large and small. He demanded that Chase, who was afforded no place to sit or even a table to place his papers, be given a chair when he requested one.[25] One newspaper wrote that Burr had conducted the proceedings with the "impartiality of an angel, but with the rigor of a devil." Burr's decision to respect the rule of law was at least partially responsible for swaying a few other Jeffersonians who would otherwise have been inclined to do the president's bidding. Chase was acquitted on every count in what might fairly have been described as Jefferson's Senate.[26]

Burr may well have preserved the independence of the federal judiciary. When Jefferson's key congressional ally, the Virginian John Randolph, introduced an amendment to the Constitution to give the president power to remove any judge with congressional approval, the effort went nowhere.[27]

Still, in thwarting the designs of America's chief executive, Burr had made a permanent enemy of Jefferson. He had also made enemies out of his Democratic-Republican colleagues.

The Chase trial was the final act of Burr's national political career. On March 2, 1805, he delivered a farewell speech proclaiming his love for the Senate that left some of his fellow members in tears. Two days later, Jefferson was inaugurated for the second time, with another Founding Father from New York, George Clinton, serving as his vice president. Finished with politics at the federal level, Burr had made an attempt to run for governor of New York in 1804, which ended in failure. Now he was simply out of a job. He would ultimately head west to try his fortune there. That's when he really got into trouble.

Burr's "Glory and Fortune"

The fortunes of two onetime political allies differed greatly after the spring of 1805. Thomas Jefferson continued to serve as president of the United States, while Aaron Burr had struck out for the new nation's western territories in order to start fresh, make more money, and perhaps even restore glory to his name.

Jefferson had been kept apprised of his disgraced former vice president's various sojourns out west, which had included an attempt to build a canal on the Ohio River. From time to time more sinister rumors emerged, suggesting that the notorious Burr was plotting some sort of coup. According to these rumors (and the newspapers that reported on them), the prodigal son would return to the Potomac, perhaps with a ragtag army in tow.

Only a year earlier, Burr had visited the Executive Mansion to dine with Jefferson. Ostensibly, Burr had sought to brief the president on his travels. But Jefferson was convinced that Burr's primary motive was to assure Jefferson that the rumors were false.

If Jefferson was ever inclined to believe his (in)famous "frenemy," then the letter that came into his possession in October 1806 left him with no doubt about Burr's true intentions. The letter had been sent by General James Wilkinson, commander of the Army of the United States, who was a longtime acquaintance of Burr's going back to the Revolutionary War. Indeed, it had been Burr who urged Jefferson to appoint the man as governor of the Louisiana Territory.[28]

Wilkinson, long known by Jefferson and others as a man of questionable character (he had once sought to pull Kentucky and Tennessee out of the Union), had sent the president a copy of a "cipher letter" written in code, insisting that it had originally been written by Burr. Dated July 29, 1806, the letter spoke of plans to gather men and supplies to move down the Ohio River in mid-November and proceed to New Orleans. Wilkinson alleged that Burr was raising an army of seven thousand and intended to "revolutionize" the territory. According to Wilkinson, who had himself been involved with this plot before allegedly having a change of heart, Burr's plan was to lead an armed conflict against the United States. The letter, supposedly written by Burr (at times in the third person) stated in part:

> *I (Aaron Burr) have obtained funds, and have actually commenced the enterprise. Detachments from different points under different pretences, will rendezvous on the Ohio, 1st November. Every thing internal and external favours views; protection of England is secured.... Wilkinson shall be second to Burr only....*
>
> *Burr guarantees the result with his life and honour, the lives, the honour and fortunes of hundreds, the best blood of our country: Burr's plan of operations is to move rapidly from the falls on the fifteenth of November, with the first five hundred or one thousand men, in light boats, now constructing for that purpose....*
>
> *[O]n receipt of this send Burr an answer; draw on Burr for all*

expenses, &c. The people of the country to which we are going are
prepared to receive us. . . .

The Gods invite to glory and fortune: it remains to be seen,
whether we deserve the boon. . . .[29]

There were some unresolved issues regarding the letter's prove-
nance. For one, Wilkinson had sent only a copy—which he claimed
to have decoded and written out himself—instead of the original.
(The encoded original, as it turned out, was not written in Burr's
own handwriting, and the decoded text did not match Burr's writing style.)[30] But it was enough to satisfy the president. This letter,
Jefferson firmly believed, was the evidence he needed to finally
show the world that Aaron Burr was a scoundrel, a reprobate, and
a traitor to the nation, which was not yet three decades old. The
man deserved to be hanged. Now Thomas Jefferson was going to
make sure that happened.

"This Scene of Depravity"

Jefferson had taken one last glance at the document before affixing
his signature. He knew that the message he would send to the
House and Senate on January 22, 1807, would soon spread across
the country and become a national sensation. But he felt duty-
bound to press his case against his old enemy—in words that did
not spare any drama—as he described "This Scene of Depravity."[31]

It was in "the latter part of September," Jefferson informed the
nation, that he received "intimations that designs were in agitation
in the western country, unlawful and unfriendly to the peace of the
Union; and that the prime mover in these was Aaron Burr, heretofore distinguished by the favor of his country."[32]

The chief executive added a note of judiciousness: "The mass of what I have received, in the course of these transactions, is voluminous, but little has been given under the sanction of an oath, so as to constitute formal and legal evidence." He went so far as to admit that much of the evidence amassed amounted to "a mixture of rumors, conjectures, and suspicions, as render it difficult to sift out the real facts, and unadvisable to hazard more than general outlines, strengthened by concurrent information, or the particular credibility of the relater."[33]

It was, he felt, a masterful prosecution—with just the right blend of outrage, umbrage, and sincerity—and it did not occur to him for a moment that he might have overstepped his role as leader of the nation to become the overzealous prosecutor of a political foe. While key witnesses had not yet been placed under oath, Jefferson still insisted in his message that there could be no doubts as to any conclusions to be drawn about a man he labeled a "criminal." Indeed, Jefferson asserted, his former vice president's "guilt is placed beyond question."[34]

Of that, he believed, there could be—and there would be—no doubt. He had been stymied before in an attempt to put an enemy on trial—when Burr presided over Samuel Chase's trial in the Senate. Jefferson did not intend to be stymied again. Of course, much would depend on the jurist who would end up trying the case.

Judiciary Versus Jefferson

As he gazed upon the scene unfolding in Richmond, the reticent man with the studious expression and graying hair took a deep breath. He had been involved in many important cases during his impressive career on the federal bench. But to Chief Justice John Marshall, the Burr trial, which began in Richmond, Virginia, on May 22, 1807, was the most unpleasant one. Indeed, he felt it was perhaps the most unpleasant case "ever brought before a judge in this or perhaps in any country which affected to be governed by laws."[35] He knew a political vendetta when he saw one; in fact, he'd been dealing with Jefferson's attacks on the judiciary from his first day in office.

Marshall's tenure as chief justice coincided with the ascent of Jefferson to the White House. Indeed, it could be argued that the outgoing John Adams appointed Marshall to the High Court as his last, best effort to undermine the Jeffersonian version of democracy: local, egalitarian, and dead-set against any accumulation of power, whether economic or political. From the start, Marshall worked to preserve the Federalists' central institutions, such as Alexander Hamilton's national bank. He insisted on the sanctity of the courts against efforts by Jeffersonians to compromise—at least in his view— the judiciary's independence and supremacy on constitutional questions. For one, he urged his colleagues on the Supreme Court to support a single majority opinion in all cases—rather than having each individual justice author a separate opinion—to give the Court's rulings the kind of legitimacy that can be achieved only through unanimity.[36] Also, Marshall had written the 1803 landmark ruling in *Marbury v. Madison*, in which the Supreme Court overturned an act of Congress as unconstitutional for the very first time.[37] By so doing, Marshall had acquired many political enemies.

The scene in Richmond had become chaotic. Drawn to the city by sensational headlines, spectators clogged the courthouse, which required moving the trial to the larger State House. Orators from all stripes were having their day. One particularly vocal Burr advocate denouncing Jeffersonian overreach was a rough and bushy-haired Tennessean named Andrew Jackson.[38] Another attention grabber was the beautiful young woman Theodosia Burr, who hung near her father's side.

Nearly everyone had come to know of Thomas Jefferson's direct involvement in Burr's case. The president was rumored to be advising the team of prosecutors, led by George Hay. Jefferson had given Hay blanket pardons to use, at Hay's unfettered discretion, to secure witnesses willing to testify in support of the prosecution. (By the time he had finished, Hay had assembled 140 such witnesses.)

Burr's defense team, in turn, included such notables as Benjamin Botts, Charles Lee, Edmund Randolph, John Wickham, and Luther Martin, a delegate to the Constitutional Convention. Martin made no secret of his friendship with Burr or of his contempt for the dictatorial tactics of Thomas Jefferson. And as the trial continued, Martin stood before Marshall with an extraordinary request.

The bulk of the case against Burr in the alleged plot to attack the United States rested on the letter President Jefferson had received from an alleged co-conspirator, General Wilkinson. Martin argued that Burr was entitled to see the entire text of the Wilkinson letters and demanded that a subpoena be issued to the president to obtain it.

"The President has undertaken to prejudge my client by declaring 'of his guilt there can be no doubt,'" Martin maintained, carefully turning the case into a referendum against what the defense characterized as Jefferson's personal agenda. "He has assumed the knowledge of the Supreme Being himself, and pretended to search the heart of my highly respected friend. He has proclaimed him a traitor. . . . He has let slip the dogs of war, the hell-hounds of prosecution, to hunt down my friend. And would this President of the United States, who has raised all this absurd clamor, pretend to keep back the papers which are wanted for this trial, where life itself is at stake? It is a sacred principle, that in all such cases, the accused has the right to all the evidence which is necessary for his case."[39] (Jefferson, for his part, wrote to Hay to suggest that Luther Martin himself—"that bulldog"—must be part of the conspiracy. He suggested that perhaps Martin, too, ought to be prosecuted for the concealment of Burr's treason, "at the least."[40] Hay declined to pursue any such charge against Burr's attorney.)

Answering Martin's request before a packed room of spectators, Marshall ruled that he had "no choice" but to issue the subpoena compelling the president to turn over the letters in their entirety. Jefferson, of course, had no intention of doing anything of the sort. When Jefferson heard of Marshall's demand, his mind wandered to core constitutional questions—specifically, to the respective powers and privileges of each branch of government. In a letter the following day, Jefferson observed that "the leading feature of our Constitution is the independence of the Legislative, Executive, and Judiciary of each other," before concluding darkly that "none are more jealous of this than the Judiciary."

Then came the venom: "But would the Executive be independent of the Judiciary if he were subject to the *commands* of the latter, and to imprisonment for disobedience; if the smaller courts could bandy him from pillar to post, keep him constantly trudging from north to south and east to west, and withdraw him entirely from his executive duties?"

Jefferson was not about to be commanded by anyone as long as he had any say in the matter—and because he was the president, he had a great deal of say. Jefferson saw it as his solemn duty to rid the country—and himself—of the troublesome Burr. He was certainly not about to let some judge (even if he was the highest in the land) infringe on the powers of the presidency and get in his way.

A key moment in his quest came on June 15, with the arrival of his star witness. General Wilkinson, the centerpiece of the legal drama before the nation, clearly intended to make the most of his moment as the center of attention. He was dressed in an elegant uniform that some claimed was of his own design. Upon seeing him enter the room, Wilkinson would later recall, the defendant

Burr "averted his face, grew pale, and affected passion to conceal his perturbation." That might have been a description best suited to Wilkinson's own agenda; it was not, however, how other onlookers described the scene as it unfolded.

The famed writer Washington Irving, then a young reporter who traveled from New York to Richmond to cover the trial, wrote: "Wilkinson strutted into court . . . swelling like a turkey-cock." A contemptuous Burr, seated beside his lawyers, refused to look at his accuser—that is, until he was directed to do so by Chief Justice Marshall. As Irving described the exchange: "The whole look was over in an instant; but it was an admirable one. There was no appearance of study or constraint in it; no affectation of disdain or defiance; a slight expression of contempt played over his countenance."[41]

The testimony against Burr was faulty from the start. There was no evidence that Burr had planned a military action against the United States, Marshall concluded, leading to one of the charges' being quickly dismissed.

The case wilted further when one of the most damning anecdotes involving Burr was dismantled. The prosecutors placed Burr on Blennerhassett Island in the Ohio River for a discussion contemplating the conspiracy, but evidence adduced by the defense established that Burr was in fact some one hundred miles away at the time in question. Toward the end of the case, even prosecutor Hay reported to Jefferson that his confidence in Wilkinson's credibility as a witness was "shaken if not destroyed."[42] Others believed it was Wilkinson, more than Burr, who had plotted treason. General Wilkinson, noted one historian, was "the most consummate artist of treason that the nation ever possessed."[43]

Chief Justice Marshall had made the crucial determination that two witnesses must testify that Burr had committed the "overt Act" of treason required by the Constitution (Article III, Section 3,

Clause 1). The government was never able to produce two witnesses to that effect, and on September 1, 1807, Aaron Burr was acquitted of treason. Though he might well have conspired against the United States in thought and speech, no "overt Act" meant no conviction. Thomas Jefferson's former vice president and longtime nemesis was a free man. The president took the news predictably.

In his ire, Jefferson's thoughts turned to a man who had thwarted him in the past: John Marshall, the chief justice of the United States. Marshall had defied him again. For a brief moment, Jefferson toyed with pushing for his impeachment from the federal bench.[44] He chose to forgo that option. Instead, he unleashed his rage with the weapon that had always proved most potent to the author of the Declaration of Independence—the pen.

He wrote to General Wilkinson, whom Jefferson still held in "great esteem and respect," to complain that "the scenes which have been acted at Richmond are such as have never been exhibited in any country, where all regard to public character has not yet been thrown off." Rather than an exercise in judicial independence, Jefferson found Burr's acquittal "equivalent to a proclamation of impunity to every traitorous combination which may be formed to destroy the Union."[45]

Another letter, written a few days later, further demonstrates the threat the president felt from the judiciary: "We supposed we possessed fixed laws to guard us equally against treason and oppression," he wrote to another friend, "but it now appears we have no law but the will of a judge. Never will chicanery have a more difficult task than has been now accomplished to warp the text of the law to the will of him who is to construe it."[46]

* * *

Aaron Burr will always be remembered as the man who shot Alexander Hamilton in an early morning duel in the marshes of northern New Jersey, but he should also be remembered as one of the first victims of a chief executive bent on exacting vengeance and a federal government that can turn its mighty coercive powers against one of its own citizens. The odds stacked against one citizen, even one as prominent as a former vice president, are nearly insurmountable—nearly. Jefferson tried to stack them even more in his favor by attempting improperly to sway the judiciary. But John Marshall, the august chief justice, would not have it. Indeed, Marshall's impartial oversight of the Burr trial saved the vice president from a conviction of treason—and death.

In a dictatorial America, Jefferson might well have gotten his way. Had he done so, he would have made a mockery of the justice system, destroyed the individual rights of those who disagreed with their government, and sent an almost certainly innocent man to his death. For all those today who doubt that an American president could wield such damaging powers, this story is instructive. It reminds us that the temptation among presidents toward excess is a strong one—so strong that, for a time at least, it overcame the good judgment of one of our greatest leaders.

It is, of course, not customary to think of Thomas Jefferson—one of our most gifted and revered founders—as a scoundrel. That is precisely what makes this historical moment so gripping and important to understand. Aaron Burr's 1807 trial offered the incredible spectacle of the president of the United States publicly declaring, without benefit of trial, his own vice president as a traitor to the nation, and demanding his arrest.

But Jefferson was not satisfied simply with Burr's arrest. Throughout the trial proceedings, Jefferson refused to hand over documents to aid Burr's defense, pressured prosecutors, and badgered the judge to exact the verdict of guilt the president desired. To some historians, the episode cast a mark of shame on Thomas Jefferson's presidency and offers warnings today about unchecked abuse of presidential power.

Aaron Burr's story serves as perhaps the ultimate cautionary tale for those who do not fully understand the threat posed by vengeful and unrestrained government officials. Jefferson and his allies sought to write off Aaron Burr entirely by executing him for treason. While that may have failed, they did succeed in making him a footnote in history, famous only for the harm he caused another. Ask yourself how you first heard of Aaron Burr—as the man who struggled to successfully prove his innocence against all the government's might, or as the villain in the story of Alexander Hamilton? Perhaps Jefferson had the last laugh after all.

The rest of the forgotten founders we will meet in the following pages all sought, in their own way, to prevent this very sort of overreach and injustice. Their stories are important for all Americans to learn—lest they be written out of history for good.

CHAPTER 2

Luther Martin: Sober Analysis from a Drunk Founder

THE GENTLEMAN FROM MARYLAND WAS NOT, AS ONE HISTORIAN put it, a man "of striking appearance."[1] He was not particularly tall or short, or especially fat or thin. What might have been most remarkable about Luther Martin, to colleagues such as George Washington and John Adams, was not his physical attributes, but his manner. Martin, present at the creation of the U.S. Constitution, was disheveled and long-winded. He was a man, a contemporary noted, who "never speaks without tiring the patience of all who hear him."[2] His face, it was remarked, was "crimsoned by the brandy he continually imbibed."[3] In other words, Luther Martin, one of America's Founding Fathers, was a notorious drunk.

Of course, it was more than just his bearing that made Martin, an accomplished Maryland attorney, a perpetual irritant to many of the great men at the Constitutional Convention in Philadelphia. When he first arrived, on June 9, 1787, he immediately questioned the "secrecy" imposed on the proceedings.[4] Why, he wondered, should the convention forbid the general public, who suffered as much for independence as anyone, from knowing what was going on? He quickly identified what he believed was the reason for secrecy: to mask the true agenda of the elites gathered in Philadelphia.

The meeting, which summoned delegates from all thirteen colonies, was billed as an effort to revise the previously ratified Articles of Confederation, which had conferred limited power to a central government. But once the session was convened, Martin soon realized that what many of the delegates—including James Madison and Alexander Hamilton, among others—actually contemplated was far more ambitious and, in Martin's eyes, far more alarming. They proposed an entirely new governing document that would remedy what many of the delegates—the Federalist faction—saw as the biggest shortcoming of the Articles of Confederation: the lack of strong federal authority.

Those who opposed such a move found themselves significantly outnumbered and outmaneuvered by such prominent national figures as George Washington and Benjamin Franklin. That didn't deter Martin from speaking out, who declared that the delegates should not "suffer our eyes to be so far dazzled by the splendor of names, as to run blindfolded into what may be our destruction."[5]

Why such harsh words? Martin, like many who became known as the Anti-Federalists, believed that the new document being considered—what would become known as the Constitution of the United States—would lead the young republic on a path that would trample on individual rights. This new central authority they were attempting to create had the potential to take on dictatorial powers, much like the monarchy from which they had just separated. Martin warned that the office of President of the United States—as the Federalists envisioned it—would wield authority that could make its holder "a king in everything but name."

Martin was the original and most outspoken Anti-Federalist. And he was among the first great defenders of state sovereign authority and federalism—the understanding that under the Constitution, federal powers (while more expansive than Martin would have preferred) are "few and defined" and those reserved to the states are "numerous and indefinite." Similarly, he fought for transparency in government proceedings. And, despite being a slaveholder himself, he fought against slavery.

Ultimately, these were fights that he would lose—but his lessons lived on even in defeat.

"The Notorious Reprobate Genius" Meets a "Very Respectable Character"

In 1772 Luther Martin, then a young lawyer fresh from passing his Virginia bar exam, went in search of a place to set up his practice. In the capital at Williamsburg, he found more than he bargained for. He found the seeds of revolution.

Williamsburg, the royal seat of colonial Virginia, was a city so modern and thriving that it could easily have passed for a small city in Great Britain. In 1772 it was presided over by Virginia's governor, Lord Dunmore, who lived in a palace and was a loyal representative of His Majesty King George III. But outside the walls of Dunmore's palace, among the people, something was afoot.

Out in the cobbled streets, a rage for revolution seethed. Yes, on the streets of the most important city in the colony you could find the landed gentry and wealthy merchants bedecked in the latest London fashions ferried around inside ornate carriages. But there were many others, too—the penniless ruffians and rowdy drunkards. In between these groups fell the vast majority of colonists— the humble yeoman farmers, craftsmen, and traders—who simply wanted to go about their lives and their business with the same rights guaranteed to any citizen of His Majesty's empire.

But by 1772, something had changed across all swaths of the American colonial populace, and Williamsburg was no exception. Members of every class, from the wealthy landowners to the local roustabouts, were recoiling against what they saw as increasing efforts by the King and Parliament to tighten their grip on their colonial cousins. The appetite for rebellion was growing. It was in America's taverns and inns where the fire of revolt burned hottest—and was often expressed most vociferously.

Luther Martin was one such rabble-rouser. Slovenly dressed and nearly always drunk, Martin had moved to the oppressively thick, humid heat of Williamsburg while Virginia's legislature was in session. He was in search of work—and trouble.

His alcohol consumption followed a very scientific pattern. "In the heat of summer my health requires that I should drink in abundance to supply the amazing waste from perspiration," Martin once explained, without apology. The style in which he delivered his strong opinions and brilliant insights was less straightforward.

"This Gentleman possesses a good deal of information, but he has a very bad delivery, and so extremely prolix [verbose, rambling], that he never speaks without tiring the patience of all who hear him," said William Pierce, who served with Martin at the Constitutional Convention. Later, the nineteenth-century historian Henry Adams would describe Martin as "the rollicking, witty, audacious Attorney General of Maryland, drunken, generous, slovenly, grand . . . the notorious reprobate genius."

Martin was as genuinely passionate as he was so often drunk. Argument was approached with the same passion and zeal that he demonstrated in his imbibing. He was relentless in the pursuit of what he believed was right. But he also held very different views from many of his fellow revolutionaries. For instance, George Washington—whom Martin respected immensely—and James Madison would ultimately become ardent champions of a strong, unifying federal government. Martin could never be convinced to see things their way. He wanted nothing whatsoever to do with such a powerful centralized government. To him, that would be trading the yoke of one tyrant for the yoke of another—only one that would not be separated by an ocean. He believed that the states should come together to frame a loose federation only for the most fundamental—and strictly limited—purposes.

And, he argued, the only entities that could keep such a powerful, centralized government in check would be the states acting jealously to guard their own rights and powers. No amount of power or rights could be given to individual citizens that would successfully hold back the deluge of tyranny that would flood upon them if a federal government were allowed to hold more power than the individual states.

Now, in the ferment of pre-revolutionary Williamsburg, Luther Martin met a kindred spirit. There is no precise record of his first meeting with Patrick Henry, but it probably occurred in the boozy confines of a tavern in Williamsburg. Martin later remembered Henry as one of the "very respectable characters" who enlivened his stay in Williamsburg.[6] The two men, hailing from colonies that shared a border but remained vastly different—tiny Maryland and massive Virginia—likely talked about the evils of a powerful centralized government and the imperative of maintaining the primacy and sovereign authority of the states. It would have been a true meeting of minds.

The Declaration of Independence was still four years away, the Articles of Confederation were five years away, and the Constitutional Convention fifteen years away. But in a crucial debate on the future of the independent states, the two men would find themselves in perfect agreement. Martin and Henry would emerge as two prominent defenders of the Articles of Confederation, and thus two of the fiercest opponents of the Constitution.

When that Constitution took form fifteen years later, Patrick Henry—who did not attend the Constitutional Convention in

Philadelphia—stood up to argue against it. "The middle and lower ranks of people have not those illuminated ideas which the well-born are so happily possessed of; they cannot so readily perceive latent objects," Patrick Henry would later state at Virginia's ratifying convention in 1788.[7] "The microscopic eyes of modern statesmen can see abundance of defects in old systems; and their illuminated imaginations discover the necessity of a change."[8]

Like Martin, Henry saw no need whatsoever to fiddle with the perfectly adequate Articles of Confederation.

And, like Martin, Henry was an early and ardent advocate for state sovereign authority, arguing that the founders who produced the document in Philadelphia did not have a moral mandate—or even the legal authority—to speak for the people.

"What right had they to say, 'We, the people' . . . instead of 'We, the states?'" Patrick Henry demanded during his state's ratifying convention.[9]

"States are the characteristics and the soul of a confederation," Henry insisted. "If the states be not the agents of this compact, it must be one great, consolidated, national government, of the people of all the states."[10]

Henry left delegates at that ratifying convention with a stark warning, first flagged in Philadelphia by Martin himself:

"If a wrong step be now made, the republic may be lost forever," he said.[11]

But all of those fights were still far off in 1772, when those two champions of state sovereign authority and skeptics of consolidated federal power—Luther Martin and Patrick Henry—both found themselves in Williamsburg. While Martin's political path would eventually take him to Philadelphia and Henry's would not, the men remained ideological compatriots to the end. Even though Martin participated in the debates around the Constitution's formation, once the document was put before the states, Martin, like Henry, would vociferously argue against it—and against the secretive manner in which it was conceived.

"Powers Ought to Be Kept Within Narrow Limits"

On June 9, 1787, Luther Martin was considerably older and wiser than he'd been when he'd met Patrick Henry fifteen years earlier. Since 1772 the shape of the world had changed. Like Henry and many other great minds of their generation, Martin had added his efforts to the patriot cause. He had eventually settled in Maryland, where he joined revolutionary groups and became the state's attorney general in 1778. He even joined a militia cavalry unit and rode south to join the fight in Virginia. The law remained his private and public passion. He maintained his own successful practice but continued to devote himself to the legal affairs of his beloved home state as attorney general. In 1787 the Maryland legislature decided to send Martin and his considerable legal talents to Philadelphia as a delegate to what became the Constitutional Convention.

On June 9, 1787, he entered the ornately paneled Assembly Room at the Pennsylvania State House—which would later become known as Independence Hall—for the first time.

He was late.

The convention had already been under way for two weeks, with most of the other players fully engaged in their political games. Martin looked around and saw them, deep in conversation with one another or making notes, sometimes casting occasional wary glances at rivals or allies across the room. There was the short, plucky James Madison; the portly but brilliant Benjamin Franklin; and, of course, there was George Washington, president of the convention, who seemed to tower (literally and figuratively) over everyone else. The great general had been there since day one and would remain to the very end.

The next day, a Sunday, the convention went into recess, and Martin was grateful for the chance to catch up. He took the opportunity to examine the journals of the debate thus far. He pored over the minutes of the discussion and interrogated fellow delegates about everything he had missed in the early weeks of the convention.

Even after he had digested the reports on the earlier proceedings, Martin did not see any reason to take the convention by storm. Instead, he gave himself more time to discern the lay of the political landscape by keeping quiet and gaining a sense of where his fellow delegates stood.

As he would later recall: "I attended the convention many days without taking any share in the debates, listening in silence to the eloquence of others, and offering no other proof that I possessed the powers of speech, than giving my yea or nay when a question was taken."[12]

But as the reality of what the convention might accomplish began more fully to dawn on him, Martin stayed silent, but for a different reason. One historian would later note that "Martin was, uncharacteristically, 'silent in disbelief at what he had heard.'"[13] In short order, that disbelief turned to sheer horror. The Articles of Confederation were not being adjusted; they were being replaced. The push for a strong central government, as outlined in the Virginia Plan presented earlier in the convention—before Martin's arrival—was now driving the debate.

When this became clear, Luther Martin realized that he could not stay silent for long. Soon he would regain his voice and run it—literally—until it was raw in voluble opposition to the federal monstrosity that was slowly, ominously taking shape in Philadelphia.

Martin would charge later that his fellow delegates "appeared totally to have forgot the business for which we were sent." In Martin's view, they "had not been sent to form a government over the inhabitants of America, considered as individuals." He felt that his fellow delegates had forgotten that "the system of government we were intrusted to prepare, was a government over these thirteen States." Instead, Martin was horrified to discover, they "adopted principles which would be right and proper only on the supposition that there were no State governments at all."[14] The state governments were being shunted aside in favor of centralized federal power, and Martin would have none of it.

Republican government, he argued, was "only suited to a small and compact territory" such as a state. He fearfully predicted that the federal Leviathan that would emerge from the Constitutional Convention would become an unmanageable behemoth whose growth the states (and therefore the people) would be powerless to control. The only way to keep the federal monstrosity in check would be to limit more strictly the authority of the federal government, thus guaranteeing the right of the people to govern themselves locally in all but a few areas.

The idea was not that state governments were and would forever be infallible. The overriding concern, rather, was that unchecked power threatened liberty. As power becomes more concentrated, it becomes more difficult to control. Preserving the sovereignty of the states prevents any one person or entity from accumulating too much power and thereby threatening liberty. Problems in government like corruption and harmful policies are easier to detect and eliminate in a state government—one whose officers live and work close to the people they serve—than in a distant, centralized government. Additionally, the nation as a whole benefits from the innovation fostered in an environment where states are allowed to govern according to their own citizens' unique ideas, needs, and local preferences.

Martin accused James Madison and his compatriots of advocating "the total abolition and destruction of state governments" in favor of a strong national government.[15]

It was no secret that Madison preferred the supremacy of the federal government to that of the states. Indeed, before the convention had even begun, in April 1787, he had communicated in a letter to George Washington his belief that a new national government should "have a negative [power], in all cases whatsoever, on the Legislative acts of the States." Madison called this "the least possible encroachment on the State jurisdictions," but nonetheless argued that "without this defensive power, every positive power that can be given on paper [by the federal government] will be evaded & defeated. The States will continue to invade the national jurisdiction, to violate treaties and the law of nations & to harrass each other with rival and spiteful measures dictated by mistaken views of interest."[16]

"This," Martin and others undoubtedly understood, "would have reduced the states to nullities."[17]

On June 27, Martin's long-building silence burst forth into a stem-winding tornado of rhetoric. He took the floor and made a speech that carried on over two days.

He spoke, according to Madison, "at great length and with great eagerness," arguing to his fellow delegates that the federal government "was meant merely to preserve the State Governments, not to govern individuals," and "that its powers ought to be kept within narrow limits." These limits were critical, he explained, because "if too little power was given to it, more might be added; but that if too much, it could never be resumed."[18] Today Martin might have remarked that once the federal genie is out of his bottle, it is difficult to put him back in.

Against this creeping federalism, Martin argued "that the States like individuals were in a State of nature equally sovereign & free."

The states' individual sovereignty could not be taken from them involuntarily, simply by creating a superseding federal structure. Rather, the states would have to decide for themselves (through their own processes, and with the support of their own people) whether to give up any sovereignty.

Martin brought in reinforcements. To support his argument for sovereign, independent states he quoted at length from the works of John Locke, the Swiss political philosopher Emer de Vattel, British Whig politician Lord Somers, and other writers.

By the time he announced that he was "too much exhausted . . . to finish his remarks," more than three hours had passed. But he assured the delegates that he would pick up where he left off the following day.

Feeling reinvigorated after an evening's rest, Martin was right back at it the following morning, arguing "with much diffuseness & considerable vehemence" that the federal government "ought to be formed for the States, not for individuals." "If the States were to have votes in proportion to their numbers of people," he told his colleagues, "it would be the same thing whether their representatives were chosen by the Legislatures or the people"—relations between the smaller and larger states would remain unequal. Martin also suggested alliances between smaller groups of individual states, remarking that he would "rather see partial confederacies take place, than the plan on the table."[19]

Drawing near to a close, Martin declared, "Happiness is preferable to the Splendors of a national Government!"[20]

According to modern historian Lynne Cheney, Martin's lengthy address "offered a theoretical basis for the small-state view, arguing that since states, like individuals, enjoyed natural equality," an equal share vote for each state was, in Martin's words, "founded in justice and freedom, not merely in policy." But any summary of Martin's speech "misses the effect it had, because it went on for two days, exhausting him and everyone who listened."[21]

The second installment of Martin's marathon speech touched off contentious debate about the relationships between large states and small states, including a response by Madison himself, which argued the best interest of the smaller states "lies in promoting those principles & that form of Govt. which will most approximate the States to the condition of counties"—that form of government being federalism.[22]

One of the many lines of scenarios that drove the Anti-Federalists to madness was when those jockeying for a strong federal constitution appeared to be clambering back into the clutches of tyranny—after all the blood, sweat, and treasure that had been spilled escaping tyranny. Martin would later complain that he was "eternally troubled" by Federalist colleagues "with arguments and precedents from the British government."[23]

As Martin had argued a few days earlier: "When the States threw off their allegiance to Great Britain, they became independent of her and each other. They united and confederated for mutual defense; and this was done on principles of perfect reciprocity. They will not again meet on the same ground. But when a dissolution takes place, our original rights and sovereignties are resumed. Our accession to the Union has been by the States."[24]

"If any other principle is adopted by this convention," he said on June 19, "[I] will give it every opposition."

Perhaps the heated debate of June 28 was what drove Benjamin Franklin to rise later in the day and lament "the small progress we have made after 4 or five weeks" as "a melancholy proof of the imperfection of the Human Understanding." Franklin thus suggested "that henceforth prayers imploring the assistance of Heaven, and its blessings on our deliberations, be held in this Assembly every morning."[25]

He may silently have been praying for Luther Martin to keep quiet. Needless to say, the gang of Federalist framers had little patience for Luther Martin and his unruly confederates. They were viewed as tedious obstructionists, and their motives were questioned as dishonorable at every turn. Elbridge Gerry was derided as a "Grumbletonian."[26] George Washington fumed in a letter to Alexander Hamilton: "The men who oppose a strong & energetic government are, in my opinion, narrow minded politicians, or are under the influence of local views."[27]

There was no room for dissent that considered the downsides of "strong and energetic" government, or the potential wisdom of these so-called local views. In their dismissal and summary railroading of the dissenters for the sake of "progress," the Federalist Founding Fathers showed a shade of single-mindedness that was not unlike that of modern-day "progressives."

"Dishonorable to the American Character"

Since Martin's three-hour filibuster in late June, the convention had seen many more contentious debates, and Martin had continued his push to weaken the federal government. During a debate on the judiciary in July, he had observed that a close alliance between the executive and judicial branches of government would be a "dangerous innovation."[28] In August, as the delegates discussed when federal troops could enter states to put down rebellions, Martin argued: "The consent of the State ought to precede the introduction of any extraneous force whatever."[29]

But on August 21, Luther Martin did the unimaginable and, quite possibly, hammered the final nail into the coffin of his own push for an exceptionally weak national government. He stood in the hot and stuffy chamber (perhaps unsteadily due to drink), the anger in his voice rising as he spoke. Then he lanced the one single festering boil that no one dared even to broach during the protracted, emotional, and highly delicate negotiations, which had morphed from updating the Articles of Confederation into something far more grand and consequential—the formation of an entirely new, powerful, and centralized federal government:

Luther Martin, himself a slaveholder, delivered a withering denunciation of slavery.

Slavery, Martin declared before his stunned fellow delegates, would poison this proposed new system—ostensibly designed to promote freedom—and ultimately lead to the new nation's undoing.

By allowing slaves to be used—albeit on a fractional basis—in the apportionment of seats in the House of Representatives, the proposed Constitution would, in Martin's view, actually encourage the continuation of slavery, and, to make matters even worse, the continued importation of new slaves would prop up the brutal transatlantic slave trade.

Martin further twisted the knife by insinuating that the prospect of more and more slaves increased the danger of slave revolts, which the new federal government would be responsible for suppressing.

But his argument was not centered on political calculations, or even on the notion that people being held as property might rise up against those who claimed to possess them. Martin went further and made a moral case against slavery.

Slavery, he told his shocked fellow delegates, "was inconsistent with the principles of the revolution," and it was further "dishonorable to the American character to have such a feature in the Constitution."[30]

If his fellow founders had any honorable principle in them, Martin argued, slavery would explicitly be abolished in the Constitution. At the very least, taxes should be levied to punish and discourage the institution.

Other delegates—even some from Northern states—came sputtering to the defense of slavery.

"Let every state import what it pleases," declared Oliver Ellsworth, a delegate from Connecticut.[31]

Roger Sherman, also representing Connecticut, argued for leaving the slavery issue alone for political purposes, because it would be "expedient to have as few objections as possible to the proposed scheme of government."[32]

John Rutledge of South Carolina joined in backing up his fellow delegates' commitment to compromise over principle.

"If the Northern States consult their interest, they will not oppose the increase of slaves, which will increase the commodities of which they become the carriers," he said.[33] In other words, slavery was a win-win for the North and the South.

Rutledge also dismissed any fears about insurrections and "would readily exempt the other states from the obligation to protect the South against them."[34]

Furthermore, he insisted, "[R]eligion and humanity had nothing to do with this question."[35]

As the debate continued into the following day, one single, lone voice in the convention hall at Philadelphia rose in defense of Martin—that of George Mason of Virginia.

"This infernal traffic originated in the avarice of British merchants," Mason said, citing the countless efforts by Virginia to outlaw the slave trade, which were thwarted by the British government.[36] "The poor despise labor when performed by slaves," Mason lamented, and further fumed that slaves "produce the most pernicious effect on manners," calling slave owners "petty tyrants."[37] Mason also joined Martin in damning the institution of slavery—and all who would defend it—as inviting "the judgement of Heaven" on the new nation.[38]

Imagine the tangle of emotions that must have roiled in the

minds of Martin (who owned six slaves) and Mason (who owned dozens) as they delivered their damning critique. But their fellow delegates were not convinced.

Ellsworth, of Connecticut, struck back, pointedly noting that he "had never owned a slave," and therefore, "could not judge the effects of slavery on character."[39] Nonetheless, the damage had been done. Martin had kicked the proverbial hornet's nest and now everybody was being stung from all sides.

"Martin's characteristically blunt assault on the institution of slavery sparked a debate that would carry over into the next day," according to the historian Bill Kauffman. "Though 'debate' is not quite the word, for as usual, Luther was trampled."[40]

Martin may have been right in predicting the devilishness that would be wrought by slavery in America, but he was almost entirely alone. The vast majority of other delegates—even those hailing from non-slave states—were hell-bent on drawing up a new federal constitution and were not about to relinquish the most potent weapon for reaching a compromise to bring in the Southern states.

Furious and fed up, Martin left Philadelphia on September 4, leaving no doubt with anyone how vehemently he opposed the gathering consensus of a federal constitution. He did not even stay long enough to formally refuse to sign the final document, as Elbridge Gerry, George Mason, and Edmund Randolph did. He was finished with this debate, and already he was turning his attention to the next fight: ratification. He still saw a chance to keep this flawed plan dominated by a strong federal government from becoming the law of the new land.

Exposing "The Dark Scene Within"

If Luther Martin had been a thorn in the sides of delegates in Philadelphia in the summer of 1787, he would by year's end become an out-of-control force of nature singularly intent on slashing all hopes for a proposed constitution that would strengthen the power of the federal government.

After his premature departure from Philadelphia, Martin argued that the delegates there had had no right to do anything other than update and propose amendments to the Articles of Confederation—they did *not* have any authority to draft a wholly new federal constitution. Further, he felt, those delegates had had no mandate to speak on behalf of (or to negotiate as representatives of) the people of their respective states. They were there only to represent the interests of each state as a whole.

But there was something else that rankled Martin to the core—something that, to him, perfectly captured just how sinister and devious the whole endeavor in Philadelphia had become. From the start of the convention, most delegates were under the agreement—or at least the impression—that all negotiations would be conducted privately, that is, in secret. The idea was to encourage the delegates to express themselves openly. Under that protection, the debate, they argued, would be more honest.

To Martin it was an affront. It seemed to suggest that they knew things would transpire that would be better concealed from the public.

In late November, Martin and the other men who had served as Maryland's representatives to the convention were summoned to Annapolis to report to the Maryland House of Delegates on progress from the summer in Philadelphia. Here, Martin would right what he saw as a terrible, terrible wrong. In a lengthy speech, Martin spilled everything. He spilled and spilled and spilled. And then he spilled some more.

It was described as a full-on filibuster, complete with conspiracy theories, sounding to many like the fiery rhetoric that preceded the Revolution.

Federalists in Philadelphia, he thundered to the Maryland delegates, were plotting "to abolish and annihilate all State governments, and to bring forward one general government, over this extensive continent, of a monarchical nature!"[41]

He impugned the conspirators for hiding in secret behind closed, locked doors to hammer out this complex new government, as if they had the right to decide what was best for everyone back home.

"I had no idea that all the wisdom, integrity, and virtue of this State, or of the others, were centered in the convention," Martin taunted.[42]

Bit by bit, Luther Martin revealed all of the problems he had with the proposed federal constitution. Big states would take advantage of smaller states. The proposed Senate would have every advantage to make laws. The president would become a king. The lack of a jury at the U.S. Supreme Court imperiled liberty of all who had business before the court!

And all of it, he harangued, would preserve "the most complete, most abject system of slavery that the wit of man ever devised."[43]

No one was spared in Martin's seemingly endless address. He even called out George Washington and Benjamin Franklin for being in on the dirty deal! But he was quick to point out that he did not wish to smear good men, but rather "to show how far the greatest and best of men may be led to adopt very improper measures through error in judgement, State influence, or by other causes."[44]

To many of those who attended the Philadelphia convention, Martin's public unloading to the Maryland legislature was a violation of their agreement to keep the proceedings private. They saw it as a dishonorable act. To Luther Martin, it was his duty to his state and family before God.

The document proposed in Philadelphia behind closed doors,

Martin concluded, was so destructive to Maryland that he didn't mind being ruined if it would prevent that document from going into effect:

"I would cheerfully sacrifice that share of property with which Heaven has blessed a life of industry," he proclaimed. "I would reduce myself to indigence and poverty, and those who are dearer to me than my own existence I would intrust to the care and protection of that Providence, who hath so kindly protected myself, if on those terms only I could procure my country to reject those chains which are forged for it."[45]

Though ultimately futile, Martin's attempt at sabotage did not die quietly. The entirety of his speech would be printed—"serially and revised"—over the following three months in Maryland newspapers and reprinted in a pamphlet he distributed called *The Genuine Information*.[46]

In the pamphlet, Martin went even further in excoriating the evils concocted in Philadelphia, giving a searing—and some would say prescient—analysis of what would happen to powerful senators who were not subject to term limits.

"If he has a family, he will take his family with him to the place where the government shall be fixed; that will become his home, and there is every reason to expect, that his future views and prospects will center in the favors and emoluments of the general government," Martin wrote. The senator, he argued, would be "lost to his own State."[47]

Anti-Federalists far and wide would herald Martin's words as revelations.

"He has laid open the conclave, exposed the dark scene within, developed the mystery of the proceedings, and illustrated the machinations of ambition," wrote a Pennsylvania Anti-Federalist. "His public spirit has drawn upon him the rage of the conspirators, for daring to remove the veil of secrecy, and announcing to the public the mediated, gilded mischief."[48]

In the end, Luther Martin and his Anti-Federalist crusaders would fail to thwart the ratification effort. Their hopes for a confederacy would die, and a federal republic with a centralized government would be born. But not before fate would have one more laugh at Martin.

The following April, Maryland convened its constitutional ratifying convention. Federalists and Anti-Federalists gathered and hashed out their differences.

But there was one noted Anti-Federalist who was silent. Luther Martin, who had preached the longest and loudest about the evils of the proposal hatched in Philadelphia, was struck down by laryngitis.

Given Martin's penchant for loquaciousness, one observer noted, Martin's silence at such a crucial juncture for the federal Constitution likely "saved a great deal of time & money to the state."[49]

On April 28, 1788, Martin's beloved Maryland would become the seventh state to ratify the new Constitution that provided for a large and powerful federal government.

And so Luther Martin's objections were ignored, marginalized, and rolled over as the new Constitution marched toward ratification until it became the law of the land. He fought against secrecy, he fought against great power concentrated in the executive branch, and he fought for state checks against federal power.

One of his causes was enshrined as part of the Bill of Rights in the Tenth Amendment, which declared that "powers not delegated to the United States by the Constitution, nor prohibited by it to the States, are reserved to the States respectively, or to the people," but as the federal administrative state expanded over two centuries, this provision became easily trampled. Certain presidents in our history sought to expand the powers of the executive branch, and most of the time they succeeded. And as this expansion occurred, the transparency that Martin so valued continued to suffer.

Martin would go on to have a successful law practice and serve thirty years as Maryland's attorney general, which today remains the longest such record in the state's history.[50] In retirement, he lost none of his vigor. He nursed hot feuds with other hated contemporaries, including Thomas Jefferson, and never shied away from wading into broiling controversies.

In his thriving law practice, Martin most famously won an acquittal in the impeachment trial of his close friend Supreme Court Justice Samuel Chase. He also served on the defense team for Aaron Burr's trial for treason. Through it all, he never gave up his taste for booze.

Once, when a client wanted Martin's capable legal services—minus the drunkenness—he offered to hire Martin on the condition that he not drink during the trial. Eager for the fee, Martin agreed. Then he soaked a loaf of bread in brandy and kept that—instead of a bottle—on hand during the trial, which he won.[51]

But, in the end, Luther Martin's most epic battles were the ones he lost—the stands he took during and after the Constitutional Convention against all-powerful federal authority, against slavery, and against a government that operated behind closed doors. Eventually, Martin's assertion that slavery was "dishonorable to the American character" was indeed written into the law of the land, but only after many more decades of pain and conflict. The objections to concentrated federal power, as raised by Martin and his like-minded colleagues, were dismissed as "narrow minded" by leaders like Washington. History is, after all, written by the victors—and hardly any individual epitomizes that descriptor more than George Washington. And so, Luther Martin went down in history as a long-winded, drunken contrarian.

However, the struggles Luther Martin waged against federal overreach and secretive government are far from over. We fight them still. The federal government spends nearly $4 trillion each year—more than the combined expenditures of all state and local governments, and roughly twenty cents out of every dollar that moves through the American economy. Many of our laws (most of them by some measures) are written not by elected lawmakers but by unelected, unaccountable bureaucrats. The sheer volume of money and power in Washington is such that it is extremely difficult for the people (and even the government itself) to fully comprehend and monitor the activities of the U.S. government.

Thus, the sheer size and complexity of the government itself becomes the facilitator of overreach and secrecy. As James Madison noted in *Federalist* number 62:

> *It will be of little avail to the people, that the laws are made by men of their own choice, if the laws be so voluminous that they cannot be read, or so incoherent that they cannot be understood; if they be repealed and revised before they are promulgated, or undergo such incessant changes that no man, who knows what the law is today, can guess what it will be tomorrow. Law is defined to be a rule of action; but how can that be a rule, which is little known, and less fixed?*[52]

Complexity is fundamentally at odds with a limited, republican form of government, in large part because it obscures the operations of government and thereby thwarts accountability.

On more occasions than I can count, I have seen the American people harmed by things that could never pass political muster but for the size and complexity of the federal government. One example of that occurred during the wee hours of October 30, 2015. While the American people slept, their representatives in the Senate launched a raid on the Social Security Trust Fund. It fell to those of us who saw this move for what it was—a theft under cover of darkness—to "illustrate the machinations of ambition" as Luther Martin did. Politicians of both parties must be held accountable. But it's hard to hold them accountable when, as happened in October 2015, the staggering size, cost, and complexity of the government make it far too easy to keep secret something as significant as a raid on the Social Security Trust Fund. Even the media fell into this trap, giving very little attention to the raid. (I did, however, release a short video on social media highlighting an objection raised by Senator Rand Paul; as I write this, that video has been viewed more than 76 million times.)

Luther Martin clearly did not care about popularity—he never let it get in the way of his speaking the truth. What he cared about was staying faithful to "the principles of the revolution," and he was far from the only one. Before, during, and after the meeting of the delegates at Philadelphia, many Americans stood up and questioned whether the newly formed government was attempting to gather as much power as the old colonial power had.

Among these, one of the most powerful and witty voices came from someone who was not even allowed to vote. But she wasn't going to let that stop her.

CHAPTER 3

Mercy Otis Warren: The Woman Who Blocked an American King

At the time of our nation's founding, women, sadly, were neither permitted to vote nor to hold public office. Notwithstanding these barbaric restrictions, certain women played a surprisingly pivotal role in the founding of the American Republic. Mercy Otis Warren stands out among them. Casting deference and a whole host of societal traditions to the wind, she became a staunch and influential advocate of liberty, warning her fellow Americans of the dangers that accompany an excessive accumulation of government authority. And although the price she paid for the cause was both substantial and unusually painful, she never relented. Like Luther Martin, Mercy stuck to her principles through thick and thin, and made plenty of waves (and enemies) in the process.

At a time when women were generally expected to confine themselves to running a household, never pausing to worry about "worldly" matters, Mercy Otis was more educated than most of the men in her social circle. At a time when women were supposed to defer to their husbands, Mercy Warren and her husband, James, treated each other as equals, respecting each other as individuals and intellectuals, and even going into political battles side by side. At a time when women were supposed to remain demure and quiet, Mercy Warren made her opinions known in no uncertain terms.

A talented writer, she never shied away from controversy, whether she was cranking out politically charged dramatic works or declaring her views on the new U.S. Constitution. Underlying much of her work was a consistent theory—that the people deserved to be protected from their government, even if that government was being founded as a new republican experiment. A strong central government with a powerful executive was not the best guarantor of our individual freedoms, Warren felt, and she remained alert for any monarchist leanings among our nation's leaders. This principled position won her fierce opposition among idealistic republicans, and it even led to a painful conflict with John Adams, one of her oldest (and most powerful) friends. It should hardly come as a surprise, then, that while Adams is a towering figure in American history, comparatively few Americans are familiar with Mercy Otis Warren.

However, Warren did not seek controversy for its own sake. She was driven by a deeper patriotism. This led her to fight for the American colonies' independence from Britain, and the same forces drove her to make sure that the new American government did not betray the principles for which the Revolution had been launched. In many ways, the cause of freedom was a natural fit for Warren, who'd been a patriotic rebel all her life.

Growing Up Otis

The Otis children were bent over their lessons and scribbling away with their quills, fully engaged in the work their tutor had assigned— or at least they were supposed to be. James Otis was fidgeting, not giving his work his full attention. But his younger sister Mercy— who, unlike most girls her age, received the same early education as her brothers—was not about to let him get away with slacking.

Mercy looked up from her own diligent work just long enough to shoot her older brother a stern look. Little sisters can be tough. It's true today, and it was true in the 1740s—at least in the case of *this* little sister.

Mercy Otis glared at her precocious older brother James Otis Jr., whom the family called "Jemmy." He was supposed to be preparing to enter Harvard University, the still rough-hewn province of Massachusetts Bay's premier place of education, but the admittedly bright boy had a long way to go. Mercy would drill knowledge—and the process of how to think—straight into Jemmy's head, just as she would tutor their brother Joseph as he, too, prepared for Harvard. Mercy's brothers would learn whether they liked it or not. She wasn't about to let them waste their opportunities for formal higher education—opportunities she knew only too well were unavailable to her.

Somehow, tasks that seemed difficult to others came easily to Mercy Otis. True, she had her other chores, helping her mother maintain their West Barnstable household and helping to raise the ten other siblings who followed James Jr., Joseph, and herself. Despite her mental acumen, however, she would never attend Harvard or any other of the few colleges then in existence in Britain's North American colonies. But Mercy Otis would find a way to make her education count—and to create a free nation in the bargain.

Revolution—a Family Affair

Mercy Otis was born into a prodigiously talented early American family. We will meet her brother James Otis Jr. elsewhere in this book, attacking the British Crown's tyrannical "writs of assistance" in a court case that led to the drafting and ratification of the Fourth

Amendment. Another brother, Joseph, became a brigadier general in George Washington's often-embattled Continental Army. Yet another brother, Samuel Allyne Otis, served as quartermaster of that same army, Speaker of the Massachusetts House of Representatives, and a member of the Second Continental Congress that operated under the old Articles of Confederation. Thanks to John Adams's patronage in April 1789, he became the first secretary of the United States Senate, serving there for twenty-five years. Samuel's son, Harrison Gray Otis, became one of the wealthiest men in the new nation, a member of the new Congress, and a leading Federalist.

But Mercy Otis Warren—scribe of the Revolution, playwright, and fierce defender against "monarchical" tendencies in the early republic—would stand out among them.

Born on September 14, 1728, in Barnstable, Massachusetts, she was the third of Colonel James Otis's thirteen children and his eldest daughter. Mercy was not formally educated, though she attended sessions with her brothers and a private tutor while she was growing up (and even that was unusual for a girl of that era). She had, at an early age, exhibited a healthy intellect—at times more robust than that of any of the Otis boys. Perhaps more significantly, however, is that she showed the will to express it.

In November 1754, the angular Mercy married her plumpish second cousin, the Plymouth merchant-attorney James Warren. Throughout their lives the couple remained devoted to each other. "I have read one Excellent Sermon this day & heard two others," he wrote to her in June 1779, adding wryly, "What next can I do better than write to a Saint," and praising her "good Sense . . . Exalted Virtue & refined Piety."[1]

James Warren was as much a patriot as were any of the Otises. In June 1775, he took up his sabre and flintlock pistol to fight at

Bunker Hill.* He later served as president of the Massachusetts Provincial Congress, a major general in the Massachusetts militia, and as the Continental Army's paymaster general. "Your spirit I admire," Mercy once wrote to her beloved husband, "were a few thousands on the Continent of a similar disposition we might defy the power of Britain."[2]

More than words, however, were necessary to win a nation's freedom. There comes a time when blood counts for more than ink. Warren family patriotism could, and did, demand truly terrible costs—including that of a mother's tears. In the summer of 1780, Mercy's second son, Winslow Warren, fell into the hands of the British when they captured the ship on which he was attempting to sail to Europe. Although Winslow survived, spending the war in London and later on the Continent, the Royal Navy was not through with the Warrens. In May 1781, the thirty-six-gun American frigate *Alliance* traded deadly fire with the fourteen-gun British sloop HMS *Atalanta* in the North Atlantic. Cannonballs whizzed through the air. Grapeshot and shrapnel shredded the left arm of the *Alliance*'s commander, Captain John Barry, later known as the "Father of the U.S. Navy." But Barry was comparatively lucky. Also aboard Barry's *Alliance* was the eldest of Mercy Warren's five sons, Lieutenant James Warren Jr. A British cannonball cost him a leg.

Was freedom worth such terrible costs? Mercy must have asked herself that question repeatedly—not just immediately following the attacks on her family, but for the duration of her providential life.

She herself never took up arms. Instead, she took up the quill. Her husband encouraged her writing talents, impressed as he was by her "mind possessed of a Masculine Genius well stocked by phi-

---

* James Warren should not, however, be confused with Dr. Joseph Warren, who died at Bunker Hill.

losophy & Religion."[3] Mercy would prove that her mind did not need to be masculine to show its genius.

The Patriot Bard

I'll make the scoundrels know who sways the scepter.
Before I'll suffer this, I'll throw the state
In dire confusion, nay I'll hurl it down,
And bury all things in one common ruin.
Over fields of death; with hastening step I'll speed,
And smile at length to see my country bleed. . . .

Mercy Otis Warren may have smiled to herself as she scribbled these lines of dialogue for Rapatio, the central character in *The Adulateur,* the play on which she was then hard at work. It was late one night in 1772—the candle at her writing desk was burning low, and James was already sound asleep upstairs. She would allow herself just a few more moments of work, just a few more notes in her draft.

Rapatio was proving a wickedly fun character to write. He was the governor of Warren's fictional locality of Servia, which, in her play, was facing civil unrest not unlike the real-life tensions that were engulfing Massachusetts. Pompous, corrupt, and scheming, Rapatio was modeled on none other than Massachusetts' own colonial governor, Thomas Hutchinson, long a nemesis of the entire Otis family, and the piece would be a skewering satire.

These times, thought Mercy, called for powerful political salvos, not mere baubles of merriment or jocularity. But she knew her dramatic talent, and she sought to harness it for the greater cause. She had resolved to write a *political play*—a decidedly *revolutionary* play.

When *The Adulateur* was published anonymously in 1773, it was the product of every facet of Mercy Otis Warren's genius. She counted reason and logic among her weapons. But also wit, sarcasm, and ridicule. Mercy's literary arsenal employed them all. One did not want to be included among her enemies. Mercy may not have purchased ink by the barrel, but what ink she had she used with extraordinary skill and, where necessary, excoriated those who earned her enmity.

In an age when few men (and even fewer women) wrote books, she proved energetically prolific, as a correspondent (her personal letters to both John and Abigail Adams are a treasure trove of revolutionary thought), a playwright, a poet, a political polemicist, and, finally, as a major historian of the Revolution.

Mercy enthusiastically embraced the revolutionary cause from the beginning. In December 1774, she remarked to an English friend, the pioneering (but in her day, definitely controversial) British historian Catharine Macaulay, that "America stands armed with resolution and virtue; but she still recoils at the idea of drawing the sword against the nation from whence she derived her origin." But Mercy felt that the mother country felt no such compunction, arguing that "Britain, like an unnatural parent, is ready to plunge her dagger into the bosom of her affectionate offspring." At that time she had at least some faith in avoiding conflict: "But may we not hope for more lenient measures!"[4]

Mercy wielded her quill while the Continental soldiers wielded their swords on the battlefields. She penned one play after another: *The Defeat* (1773), *The Group* (1775), *The Blockheads* (1776), *The Motley Assembly* (1779), and *The Sack of Rome* (1787). Oddly enough, these plays were never meant to be performed—only to be published and read. None were melodramas or drawing room farces; all were as decidedly political as her first. By 1788, however, with the fight against

King George over, Mercy turned her mind and her pen to events no less important: the struggle over ratifying the new Constitution.

"The False Glossary of Pretended Statesmen and Superficial Politicians"

By the summer of 1787, the Revolution that Mercy had championed was over. The new nation's leading lights were hard at work in Philadelphia to draft a new governing document that would end up replacing the old Articles of Confederation, and Mercy Otis Warren was nervous.

She was hardly alone. The objections of Luther Martin of Maryland have been previously discussed, and other delegates to 1787's Constitutional Convention had serious qualms. New York's Robert Yates, a member of his state's supreme court, vociferously objected: "This [new federal] government is to possess absolute and uncontroulable power, legislative, executive, and judicial, with respect to every object to which it extends."[5] Like Martin, Yates soon departed from Philadelphia, wanting nothing to do with any new constitution. Massachusetts delegate Elbridge Gerry damned the new document as "full of vices."[6] Gerry and Virginia delegate George Mason, both of whom we will come to know in great detail later in this book, would ultimately refuse to sign the Constitution over its lack of protections for individual rights.

Mercy and James Warren shared their distress. Redcoats might no longer prowl Boston streets. Royal tax collectors armed with "writs of assistance" might no longer barge into storekeepers' shops and homes. But Mercy Warren, her eyesight fading fast but her wits as keen as ever, was still nervous about the possibility of encroaching tyranny at the hands of domestic republicans rather than agents of a foreign monarch. As she paced her drawing room, she pondered the dangers posed by any new constitution lacking specific guarantees of personal liberties.

She paused, closing her eyes to collect her thoughts before sitting down and beginning to write—not a new play, but a letter to fellow dissenter Elbridge Gerry, then still at Philadelphia.

"Does anything yet transpire from the conclave?" Mercy cautiously inquired. "Or is all yet locked up in silence and secrecy? Be it so: yet some of us have lived long enough not to expect everything great, good, and excellent, from so imperfect a creature as man . . . my own opticks will never again be deceived by the false glossary of pretended statesmen and superficial politicians, therefore [I] shall not be disappointed either at the mouse or the mountain that this long labour may produce."[7]

Mercy's anxieties about the Constitution mounted. By September 1787 she had reported to her British friend Catharine Macaulay (now Catharine Macaulay Graham): "Our situation is truly delicate & critical. On the one hand we stand in need of a strong Federal Government founded on principles that will support the prosperity & union of the colonies. On the other we have struggled for liberty & made lofty sacrifices at her shrine: and there are still many among us who revere her name too much to relinquish (beyond a certain medium) the rights of man for the Dignity of Government."[8]

Mercy's husband, James, took up the fight as well. At the time, controversial political opinions were often voiced anonymously (perhaps some of today's online commenters are simply engaging in a time-honored tradition!). Robert Yates attacked the new Constitution using the nom de plume "Brutus." Alexander Hamilton, James Madison, and John Jay penned *The Federalist Papers* as "Publius." John Adams (never known for his sense of humor) even once employed the pseudonym "Humphrey Ploughjogger."

On December 27, 1787, James Warren, writing as "Helvidius Priscus" in Boston's *Independent Chronicle*, exhorted "the old Patriots" to "come forward, and instead of secretly wrapping up their opinions within their own breasts, let them lift up the voice like a trumpet, and show this people their folly and . . . impending danger."[9]

If the Constitution as it was written did pose an "impending danger," the Warrens were going to have more than a few words to say on the subject.

Mercy Warren Makes Her *Observations*

You didn't log on to the Internet or switch on cable television in 1788 Boston to obtain breaking news of the Constitutional Convention in Philadelphia. You hiked to the nearest tavern or coffeehouse to pick up a copy of the latest newspaper to learn what—in those days of rudimentary communication—passed for the latest news.

When the latest missive on the new Constitution came out in 1788, Boston's Green Dragon Tavern would have been buzzing.

"Did you see this?" one Bostonian, a pro-Constitution Federalist, demanded as he waved a freshly printed pamphlet to catch the attention of a friend at the next table, who nearly spilled his mug of ale. "*Observations on the New Constitution, and on the Federal and State Conventions,* they call it, and it's just outrageous. It dares to claim we need something called a 'bill of rights' in our new Constitution! More confounded delays! Hang it all—we must adopt our new Constitution *now*! Blasted idlers! Pernicious! Pernicious!"

The other Federalists in the tavern murmured their assent. But none among them knew the identity of the author behind *Observations on the New Constitution*. All they knew was the pseudonym under which it had been printed: "A Columbian Patriot." Because Elbridge Gerry had emerged as one of just three delegates who refused to sign the proposed Constitution,[10] many logically assumed Gerry was the author.

They were wrong. Mercy Otis Warren's mighty pen had struck again.*

Her *Observations* attacked the proposed new Constitution left and right, giving voice to concerns that a new, strong, and distant federal government could trample the rights both of the individual states and of the people. A "many-headed monster," she called it, "of such motley mixture, that its enemies cannot trace a feature of democratic or republican extract; nor have its friends the courage to denominate it a monarchy, an aristocracy, or an oligarchy."[11] Among her observations:

> *There are no well defined limits of the Judiciary Powers, they seem to be left as a boundless ocean, that has broken over the chart of the Supreme Lawgiver, "thus far shalt thou go and no further," and as they cannot be comprehended by the clearest capacity, or the most sagacious mind, it would be an Herculean labour to attempt to describe the dangers with which they are replete. . . .*[12]
>
> *. . . The Executive and the Legislative are so dangerously blended as to give just cause of alarm, and everything relative thereto, is couched in such ambiguous terms—in such vague and indefinite expression, as is a sufficient ground without any objection, for the reprobation of a system, that the authors dare not hazard to a clear investigation. . . .*[13]
>
> *. . . There is no provision for a rotation, nor anything to prevent the perpetuity of office in the same hands for life; which by a little well timed bribery, will probably be done, to the exclusion of men*

---

* Not until 140 years later, through the research of one of her descendants, the legal scholar Charles Warren, was her authorship discovered.

of the best abilities from their share in the offices of government.—
By this neglect we lose the advantages of that check to the overbear-
ing insolence of office, which by rendering him ineligible at certain
periods, keeps the mind of man in equilibrio, and teaches him the
feelings of the governed, and better qualifies him to govern in
his turn.[14]

An overreaching judiciary. Executive orders. A permanent governing class. "Insolence of office." Her concerns may sound familiar to
us even today. Some of her strongest rhetoric emerged when she discovered the lack of protections from unlawful searches and seizures:

I cannot pass over in silence the insecurity in which we are left
with regard to warrants unsupported by evidence—the daring
experiment of granting writs of assistance in a former arbitrary
administration is not yet forgotten in the Massachusetts; nor can
we be so ungrateful to the memory of the patriots who counter-
acted their operation, as so soon after their manly exertions to save
us from such a detestable instrument of arbitrary power, to subject
ourselves to the insolence of any petty revenue officer to enter our
houses, search, insult, and seize at pleasure.[15]

This last line of attack surely must have been dearest to her
heart, alluding as it did to her own brother James's impassioned
assault on Britain's despised royal writs of assistance. James Otis's
arguments might have inspired Adams and other revolutionaries,
but as Mercy argued, what was there in this new Constitution that
would prevent officials of the new American government from overstepping the same boundaries as their British predecessors? What
was the point of a revolution against the old regime if the new one
had the potential to be just as bad? To that end, she concluded: "There

is no provision by a bill of rights to guard against the dangerous encroachments of power in too many instances to be named."[16]

She had developed the invaluable skill of losing a battle but winning a war—as did her brother James, as we will see later. Mercy Warren and her *Observations* failed to convince her own state of Massachusetts to reject the Constitution, but Bay State delegates hardly rejected all her arguments. Massachusetts' February 1788 vote on ratification was very close (187–168), and it succeeded only because Governor John Hancock (himself a delegate) proposed that ratification be accompanied by clarifying amendments, including a bill of rights.

Other states voted in the wake of Massachusetts' narrow, qualified decision. New York was a key to ratification. If it rejected the Constitution, the new nation would be geographically cut in half. The whole experiment might still fail. Anti-Federalists, others like Mercy opposed to a strong central government, shipped sixteen hundred copies of her *Observations on the New Constitution* for distribution around the battleground state.[17] In April 1788, the *New York Journal* published her arguments.[18]

In the end, New York voted for ratification—but repeated the Bay State's call for inserting highly specific guarantees of liberty into the Constitution. New York's memorandum supporting ratification (the longest by far of any state) echoed much of what was found in Mercy's *Observations*, particularly her antipathy to broad-brush searches and seizures. New York's ratification convention declared:

> *That every freeman has a right to be secure from all unreasonable searches and seizures of his person, his papers, or his property; and therefore, that all warrants to search suspected places, or seize any freeman, his papers, or property, without information, upon oath or affirmation, of sufficient cause, are grievous and oppressive;*

and that all general warrants (or such in which the place or person suspected are not particularly designated) are dangerous, and ought not to be granted.[19]

Three other states supported Massachusetts' and New York's demands, ratifying the new compact but strongly suggesting a bill of rights. The idea came to be called the Massachusetts Compromise, after the state that first proposed it, having been influenced by Mercy Otis Warren's passionate plea. That compromise—based on Mercy Warren's work—helps guarantee our civil liberties to this day.[20]

Warren Versus Adams: "Beclouded by a Partiality for Monarchy"

John Adams was enjoying his semiretirement. The former president, one of America's first elder statesmen, finally had time to putter about his Quincy, Massachusetts, farm estate, Peacefield, and he at last had time to read for pleasure. On this particular evening, he settled down before a large fire and began to tackle his old friend Mercy Otis Warren's magnum opus, her *History of the Rise, Progress and Termination of the American Revolution.* It had been out for two years, and Adams felt it was high time he got around to reading it.[21]

For quite a while the reading went well, his reactions occasionally marked by a puzzled *hmmm,* a knotted brow, or a slight smile. But . . . then . . .

Then came passage after passage regarding his career abroad and his supposed infatuation with the monarchy. Mercy Warren, it turned out, had made precious little effort to conceal her growing antipathy to her (and her late brothers') former friend. Adams fairly leaped from his chair—or, at least, as much as a man in his seventies might.

He was driven to this state by reading the most recent fruits of Mercy Otis Warren's pen. When the Constitution was ratified, she was sixty years old. Her country was independent and finally unified. Within three years, the Bill of Rights—for which she had so strongly advocated—would be adopted. Yet her role in the founding era was not finished.

She soon took on the task of chronicling the momentous times she had lived through and helped to shape, toiling for years on a massive three-volume *History of the Rise, Progress and Termination of the American Revolution, Interspersed with Biographical, Political and Moral Observations* (cost: $2.00 for the set).[22] Its first volume was not published until 1805.

This masterwork fully revealed her continuing distrust of a strong central government. And although she had always been a close friend to both John and Abigail Adams (she dedicated her 1787 play, *The Sack of Rome,* to John),[23] she found herself drifting away from his brand of politics.

True, she had become reconciled to the idea of the new federal system, even confiding to Elbridge Gerry: "If this constitution, which is now ratified, be not supported, I despair of ever having a government of these United States."[24] Yet she remained intensely distrustful of how any strong central government might devolve into something less republican and more aristocratic and autocratic— even monarchical. More than vague promises—or even constitutional amendments—might be necessary to rein in its powers. As early as April 1789 that attitude started to fray her relations with John Adams (now George Washington's vice president), warning him that "the people of America will be remarkably averse to . . . obedience to the authority they have instituted."[25]

When Mercy Warren published her monumental *History of the Rise, Progress and Termination of the American Revolution,* however, relations between the two old friends completely broke down. She came to conclude that not only had Adams been a tad too enthusiastic about adopting a constitution without a bill of rights back in 1788, but also that after so much time among the crowned heads of Europe as ambassador to Britain and the Netherlands, he had jettisoned his early republican ways and developed distinctly dangerous pro-monarchical attitudes.

She wasn't the only observer anxious about a prospective American "monarchy" or "aristocracy." Even as the Constitutional Convention struggled to produce a document, Virginia's Edmund Randolph warned, "When the people behold in the senate, the countenance of aristocracy; and in the president, the form of at least of a little monarch, will not their alarms be sufficiently raised."[26] Elbridge Gerry feared "as complete an aristocracy as ever was framed."[27] James Warren criticized John Hancock's behavior as governor of Massachusetts as offensive and alien "to the hardy and sober manners of a New England public."[28]

Such fears were only aggravated by our first presidential election. Only five states (Delaware, Maryland, New Hampshire, Pennsylvania, and Virginia) chose electors purely by popular vote.[29] Even in Mercy's own Commonwealth of Massachusetts the legislature—and not the people—selected two of its ten electors. And, of course, there remained the vexing question of who could vote. Women were still blocked from the ballot box, as were slaves and indentured servants. Even free men could find themselves disenfranchised for not owning land. In Pennsylvania only 7,383 persons voted. In Virginia it was a mere 4,333. In our first presidential contest, in which balloting was conducted from December 1788 to January 1789, only 43,782 individuals in a nation of 4 million souls cast presidential ballots.[30] Had newly freed America merely become the world's newest aristocracy?

When revolution erupted in France, Mercy Warren, like Adams's great rival Thomas Jefferson, expressed great sympathy for its goals. Adams, however, quickly distanced himself from its too violent, too democratic aspects. Essentially siding with monarchical Britain, he even engaged in an undeclared naval war, "the Quasi-War," with republican France.

But that was while John Adams was serving as president. Years later, when he settled down at Peacefield to read how Mrs. Warren had chronicled the Revolution, he was treated to passages such as the following:

> *Mr. Adams was undoubtedly a statesman of penetration and ability; but his prejudices and his passions were sometimes too strong for his sagacity and judgment. . . .*[31]
>
> *. . . After Mr. Adams's return from England, he was implicated (i.e., regarded) by a large portion of his country men, as having relinquished the republican system, and forgotten the principles of the American revolution, which he had advocated for near twenty years. . . .*[32]
>
> *. . . Mr. Adams's former opinions were beclouded by a partiality for monarchy.*[33]

Mercy Warren did not, however, let her concerns about public policy intrude upon her opinion of Adams's person. Avoiding the "politics of personal destruction," Mercy informed her readers "that notwithstanding any mistakes or changes in political opinion, or errors in public conduct, Mr. Adams, in private life, supported an unimpeachable character; his habits of morality, decency and religion, rendered him amiable in his family, and beloved by his neighbours."[34]

Such sentiments, however, failed to mollify Adams. Initially restraining his discontent behind the era's courtly manners ("Madam I never attempt to write to you but my Pen conscious of its inferiority, falls out of my hand"),[35] he was unable to hold back his simmering anger for long.

It wasn't just Mercy's allegations of monarchism that perturbed him, however; he also believed that Mercy had slighted his role during the Revolution's early years. "If Mrs. Warren is determined to be enrolled in the glorious list of libellers of John Adams," he fumed, "she is welcome."[36]

A series of letters sped back and forth between them, as fast as couriers could carry them. With each exchange, their contents grew less and less pleasant. Quarter might be asked—but not given.

Consider these excerpts, a veritable ping-pong of no-longer-concealed acrimony:

WARREN: "The lines with which you concluded your late correspondence cap the climax of rancor, indecency, and vulgarism. Yet, as an old friend, I pity you; as a Christian, I forgive you; but there must be some acknowledgment of your injurious treatment or some advances to conciliation, to which my mind is ever open, before I can again feel that respect and affection toward Mr. Adams which once existed in the bosom of MERCY WARREN."[37]

ADAMS: "If I were to measure out to others the treatment that has been meted to me, I could make wild work with some of your party. Shall I indulge in retaliation or not?"[38]

WARREN: "Criticism, in order to be useful, should always be decent."[39]

ADAMS: "Mrs. Warren, it is my opinion, and that of all others of any long experience that I have conversed with, that your *History* has been written to the taste of the nineteenth century and accommodated to gratify the passions, prejudices, and feelings of the party who are now predominant."[40] . . . But most of these have already come to a bad end and the rest will follow."[41]

She finally concluded that the former president's impassioned protestations sounded "more like the ravings of a maniac than the cool *critique* of genius and science."[42]

Whether Mercy's suspicions about Adams's closet monarchism reflected his true thinking, one doesn't have to agree with her specific position to admire her fiery belief in the American experiment and her willingness to risk all: life, fortune, sacred honor—and long-standing friendships—in its defense.

"Female Genius in the United States"

Right up until the end, the letters never stopped.

Mercy Otis's mind and pen were kept busy even in old age, answering her immense amount of correspondence. It came not just from her dearest relations and from the friends she had accumulated from nearly eight decades of an extraordinary life, but also from the famous, the talented, and the powerful on both sides of the Atlantic.

But not all of her correspondence sparked joy. Her feud with John Adams had continued. Her fellow patriot was still furious with her years after the publication of her landmark *History*.

Cherished friendships torn apart by harsh correspondence: this was the price Mercy Otis Warren paid in full for championing her principles during the birth of the American democracy.

Mercy Otis Warren was no ordinary woman, nor was she an ordinary American. Even before the new American Republic formally came into existence, she enlivened America's intellectual and political discourse with an unceasing flow of plays, poems, tracts, and nonfiction. Such was her talent as a playwright that Alexander Hamilton was later moved to remark: "In the career of dramatic composition at least, female genius in the United States has outstripped the Male."[43]

He spoke of Mrs. Mercy Otis Warren and no one else.

Even John Adams, writing about her works in 1789 before their bitter feud ignited, poignantly observed: "However foolishly some European writers may have sported with American reputation for genius, literature, and science, I know not where they will find a female poet of their own to prefer to the ingenious author of these compositions."[44]

Even if Adams never found his portrayal by Warren in her *History* to be "ingenious," their story at least has a happy ending. Though their feud continued for nearly a decade, finally, in 1812, the two old friends reconciled, thanks to the efforts of John's wife, Abigail. To commemorate this burying of the hatchet—or, in this case, the burying of weaponized pens—Abigail gave Warren two beautiful gifts, a brooch and a ring.[45] The brooch, adorned with pearls and coiled gold, contained a lock of Warren's own hair, which she had given Abigail on an earlier occasion. Embedded in the ring were pieces of both John's and Abigail's hair.[46] Exchanging locks of hair was a common custom among close friends at the time, and signified the rebuilding of bonds between these notable individuals.

The gesture came not a moment too soon. Just two years after this exchange, in 1814, Mercy Otis Warren died.

Today this "female genius of the United States" is honored at Barnstable's two-story Greek Revival county courthouse. If you walk up its finely trimmed front lawn, you will see, looking down upon you from a stately granite pedestal, a seven-foot-high bronze statue of James Otis Jr. That's not much of a surprise. Americans, after all, still quote his ringing words: "Taxation without representation is tyranny." But look to your right and there you will see a matching statue, just as high and just as grand, of Mercy Otis Warren. Attired in her colonial finery, her long gown flowing downward, her left hand brandishes a quill pen. Her right hand holds aloft a small book. It might be *Observations on the New Constitution* or one of her plays or histories. But whatever that volume may be, the message within it remains the same: liberty.

On the front side of the pedestal are carved these words:

MERCY

OTIS

WARREN

BORN W. BARNSTABLE

1728–1814

CHAMPION OF THE BILL OF RIGHTS

PLAYWRIGHT—POET—HISTORIAN

PATRIOT

Patriot, indeed.

But while Barnstable is justly proud in remembering one of its own distinguished residents, why is Mercy Otis Warren not a more widely known name associated with the Revolution? Why has her prolific literary output not earned her more lasting praise? Generations of schoolchildren can recite Longfellow's poem commemorating the midnight ride of Paul Revere, but who remembers any lines from *The Adulateur*?

Perhaps Mercy Warren sealed her fate by speaking out. She

may have championed the cause of revolution, but her zeal in pointing out the defects of the original Constitution and the lack of a bill of rights landed her firmly on the "wrong side" of one of the new nation's first major debates—a wrong side that would later be proved right. And to make matters worse, she personally enraged one of the chief proponents of a strong central government, John Adams. Adams remains well known, yet Mercy's memory has faded. It is hard to keep from wondering: What might have happened if, instead of striking out on her own, she had used her witty and incisive pen to toe the Federalist line? Perhaps, had she defended Adams and the Federalists in her *History of the Rise, Progress and Termination of the American Revolution,* it would have become a standard text. Her warnings about a bill of rights proved especially prophetic, as the push to add those ten crucial amendments to the Constitution shortly after its ratification bears out.

Indeed, the concerns that she and others felt about a strong central government were not exactly novel. They hearken back to an understanding of the way federalism is *supposed* to work—when smaller, diverse political units come together in a larger unit to act in concert by mutual consent. This was a system that had been practiced in parts of America for a very long time—even before the Revolution.

CHAPTER 4

Join or Die: Canasatego, Ben Franklin, and the Confederacy in the Wilderness

---

Our wise forefathers established union and amity between the Five Nations. This has made us formidable. This has given us great weight and authority with our neighboring Nations. We are a powerful Confederacy and by your observing the same methods our wise forefathers have taken you will acquire much strength and power; therefore, whatever befalls you, do not fall out with one another.

—Canasatego, 1744[1]

It would be a very strange thing if Six Nations of Ignorant Savages should be capable of forming a Scheme for such an Union and be able to execute it in such a manner, as that it has subsisted Ages, and appears indissoluble, and yet a like union should be impracticable for ten or a dozen English colonies.

—Benjamin Franklin, 1751[2]

If you are a student of the constitution and America's founding, you have no doubt heard of Baron de Montesquieu and John Locke, two of the most influential thinkers of the period. You've heard of the Magna Carta and the European Enlightenment. You've read how our founding generation looked back to ancient Greece and Rome and studied their political philosophies. One name you may not be familiar with is Canasatego, an Iroquois chief who played an outsized role in shaping the way at least one Founding Father thought about republican government.

The Founding Father influenced by Canasatego was, to put it mildly, one who left a lasting impression. No one typified that enterprising, experimental, and rebellious spirit that permeated the American colonies better than an ambitious Philadelphia printer named Benjamin Franklin. A man of diverse interests, Franklin had become by 1750 one of the colonies' most influential citizens. His rags-to-riches story, his ingenuity, and his quest for the "next big thing" would lead many to dub him "the first American." But this so-called first American found inspiration for a new order and a new, unified colonial government from those who had lived in America long before him.

This is the forgotten story of how the Iroquois developed one of the most unique and essential components of the future American Republic—federalism. As their own law stated:

> *Five arrows shall be bound together very strong and each arrow shall represent one nation. As the five arrows are strongly bound this shall symbolize the complete union of the nations. Thus are the Five Nations united completely and enfolded together, united into one head, one body and one mind.*[3]

While an individual arrow by itself could be broken, they became stronger when bound together.

This concept would leave an indelible imprint on the intellectually curious mind of Benjamin Franklin, who immortalized it in the most famous American political cartoon of all time: "Join, or

Die." This same idea of limited federal power—in which the individual states joined together to protect certain shared interests but preserved control over their own local affairs—was critical to the arguments that led Luther Martin, Mercy Otis Warren, and others to question the Federalists' Constitution drafted in Philadelphia.

The Great Law of Peace

The shadows of the oaks were growing long with the sun plunging toward the western horizon. With the light dimming under the canopy of leaves, Canasatego estimated that he had another fifteen minutes at most to fell his prey. He had been following his favorite game trail all afternoon in search of white-tailed deer. The meandering trail ran parallel to the sacred Susquehanna River, near the border of what would become Pennsylvania and New York. The river's silent course carved its way through the deep forest and rolling hills, narrowing occasionally into boisterous rapids. The young warrior of the Onondaga tribe had swum its depths and trodden its nearby hunting paths hundreds of times, just as he was doing this fall evening in 1723.

As he walked, careful with each step not to break a branch or to rustle leaves, his mind often drifted off. He imagined his father, and his father before him, walking the same trails, in an endless stretch of man hunting animal going back millennia. This was his people's land, and he was proud of it.

Out of the corner of his eye he saw a shadow move behind a tree. He froze. He grabbed an arrow from his quiver and gently set it on his bow. He slowed his breathing, preparing for release when the creature came into sight again. Canasatego took a cautious step forward. A branch cracked beneath his foot. He heard a loud, bloodcurdling noise—nothing like any sound he had ever before heard an animal make. It was a war cry.

Out from behind the tree stepped a man, adorned in full war paint, with his arrow drawn taut against his bow. Canasatego wondered whether he should fire before his opponent did. The other young warrior was in position to send an arrow straight into Canasatego's chest—piercing his heart if the warrior had any talent.

Both men held mirrored poses for what seemed like an eternity, taking each other in. And then they simultaneously broke out in laughter and put their bows and arrows at rest. Canasatego's would-be assailant's markings clearly showed he was a Mohawk—a friend.

The Mohawks and Onondagas had for centuries been rivals, and at times even enemies, fighting over hunting grounds. And though they were still separate peoples with fierce tribal loyalties, they were now allies as part of the Iroquois Confederacy. Canasatego had seen enough white men hunting on his lands with wood-and-metal sticks that made loud noises, and he knew that the tribes would have to band together if they had a chance of protecting their lands and their people, and preserving the Great Law of Peace.

Canasatego took pride in the resourcefulness and organizational skills of his people. His father and his father's father had passed down the story of the Iroquois Nation's founding some three hundred years earlier. The many tribes in the area had previously been divided, frequently warring in conflicts that stretched back to the beginning of time. Though he had never seen them or wandered to the great river, the great mountains, or the shining sea even farther to the west, Canasatego knew that the Native people in those distant lands still spilled blood in frequent tribal wars.

But not the Iroquois—at least not in recent history, since the Great Law of Peace had created the Iroquois Confederacy.[4] The

Great Law of Peace was a set of rules—a constitution of sorts, albeit an unwritten one. It was passed from generation to generation in the oral traditions of his people, from chief to chief and sachem to sachem. It was depicted in pictographs on wampum belts made from seashells. To the Iroquois, the Great Law of Peace was as sacred as any written constitution could ever be.

According to his people's legend, the Great Law began with the planting of the Tree of the Great Peace, a vast white pine in the heart of the Onondaga Nation. The Tree of Great Peace was the capital of the Iroquois Confederacy, located in the western reaches of what the white man dubbed the colony of New York. That was also where the Great Council met around a campfire and decided on political matters relevant to the entire confederacy of tribes. That was where leaders from the Six Nations comprising the Iroquois Confederacy—the Mohawks, the Senecas, the Oneidas, the Cayugas, the Tuscaroras, and the Onondagas—met and deliberated with great solemnity. Decisions were made only after the tribal leaders had achieved unanimity. The Great Law prescribed specific procedural rules. It allowed for vetoes and outlined the rights, responsibilities, and qualifications of each member of the confederacy. It even contained rules governing elections and impeachment.

This union bound together as brothers the Onondaga warrior Canasatego and his would-be Mohawk rival, and not only prevented a chance encounter in the wilderness from turning ugly, but kept the peace between thousands. Canasatego walked toward the Mohawk warrior with a confident, outstretched arm. He shook his hand firmly and recited the words of the Great Law of Peace that his father had taught him:

> Roots have spread out . . . one to the north, one to the west, one to the east and one to the south. These are the Great White

Roots and their nature is peace and strength. If any man or any nation outside the Five Nations shall obey the laws of the Great Peace and shall make this known to the statesmen of the League, they may trace back the roots to the tree. If their minds are clean and they are obedient and promise to obey the wishes of the Council of the League, they shall be welcomed to take shelter beneath the Tree of the Long Leaves.[5]

Also critical to the Great Law of Peace was what it *did not* do—it did not meddle in the internal governance of the constituent tribes. When the Great Council met to make important decisions, the representatives of each tribe would discuss the matter among themselves before a final verdict was rendered by the full council. Even other tribes who were absorbed into the confederacy through conquest had the right to continue to manage their own affairs, as long as they remained peaceful.[6] The idea of separate political entities uniting for common good but retaining their own rights—what later became known as federalism—did not miraculously materialize in the summer of 1787 in the State House at Philadelphia. It had been born centuries earlier in an Iroquois longhouse.

The Great Peace was the Iroquois' strength; it provided their only chance to remain united against intruders who came from across the sea—and seemed to have an insatiable appetite for land.

New City, New Opportunities

On that very same day, in a very different part of Pennsylvania, a very different young man was settling into his new home.

Sunday church bells were ringing, their leaden waves radiating outward from the city's steeples and dissipating with each of Philadelphia's perfectly square city blocks. The bells were still loud when they reached the ears of a barrel-chested seventeen-year-old walking up Market Street with nothing more than a Dutch dollar and a shilling of copper in his pocket.[7] From the confidence he exuded one would not have known that he was at once broke and a runaway. Chewing on a stale roll he had squirreled away in his bag, he was keen to strike up a conversation with anyone who crossed his path.

It was true that his gregariousness and general curiosity had gotten the best of young Benjamin Franklin back in Boston, the town of his birth. But he couldn't take that city's suffocating Puritanism and closed-mindedness. So he fled, abandoning a promising apprenticeship at his brother's newspaper business, infuriating the entire Franklin family.

While acutely aware of his empty pockets, young Benjamin confidently understood that the opportunities before him were boundless—especially in Philadelphia. The moment he stepped foot on the creaking planks of the city wharf, he was absolutely certain that he had found his adopted home. He was captivated—even spellbound—by the energy of the merchants around him, the smell of the fishmonger and the butcher simultaneously at work in their respective trades, and the raucous cacophony of German, Scottish, and Irish brogues haggling in the marketplace.

Yes, in the eyes of this new arrival, Philadelphia was a city of hardworking, tolerant, friendly, and unpretentious people. It was all intoxicating, especially when compared with straitlaced Boston.

Philadelphia—as befits its meaning, "Brotherly Love"—had been founded by William Penn in the belief that human beings could peacefully coexist in society. It was a city that, at Penn's insistence, would have no walls. He neither needed nor desired to exclude Native Americans from the city. After all, as he was preparing to establish the colony of Pennsylvania, Penn wrote to the local tribal leaders and expressed his wish to "always live together as neighbors and friends" with the Native peoples he met.[8]

The world of the Onondaga warrior, who lived by the Great Law of Peace, and the world of young Benjamin Franklin, who lived by his wits, would eventually collide in a way that would do just that.

The Colonies and the Confederacy

In the years since Benjamin Franklin arrived in Philadelphia, the colonial territories had only flourished. Naturally, that had brought the colonists into contact—and often into conflict—with their Native neighbors. On June 22, 1744, delegates from several colonies invited the Iroquois to a conference near Lancaster, Pennsylvania, to discuss relations between their peoples.

The Iroquois were known for their hospitality. So, naturally, when they were the guests, they expected their own generosity to be reciprocated. Their hosts had self-interested reasons to be generous, too; they desperately needed an alliance with their guests. The commissioners from New York, Pennsylvania, Maryland, and Virginia knew they had to return to their respective colonies with an agreement in hand.

Nothing less than the future of North America—at least its future as an English-speaking continent—hung in the balance. The French were creeping down the spine of the Appalachian ridge, along the Eastern Seaboard that marked the known boundaries of the English-speaking colonies. The French insisted that they were merely trapping beavers and expanding their trading empire, but London's representatives in the colonies knew better. They had but one option to thwart the French advance—they would have to form an alliance with the Iroquois tribes, one that could serve as a buffer between the British colonies and the still-rustic outposts established by Britain's longtime nemesis in western Europe.

The European colonists and the Indians composing the Iroquois Confederacy had an uneasy, if peaceful, coexistence. The National Park Service estimates that at one time, the Six Nations territory spread "north to the Sorel River in Canada, south to the Carolinas, west to the Mississippi, and east to the Atlantic," making them "easily the dominant Indian confederacy in the northeast and northwest areas of America."[9] But when Europeans arrived in their ships with visions of self-appointed grandeur, the Iroquois discovered that a bow and a quiver of arrows were no match for gunpowder. They were pushed west, content to inhabit the great forests and valleys west of the Blue Ridge Mountains. In 1722 a treaty ratified their understanding. There was only one problem: the mountain range understood by the Iroquois was an entirely different range—the Allegheny Mountains farther west.

Some had canoed south with the currents of the Susquehanna River. Some had hiked northward through the foothills of the Shenandoah. All told, 245 chiefs, warriors, women, and children from the Six Nations of the Iroquois had come. They had been met on the outskirts of town by Conrad Weiser, the colonies' most respected Indian interpreter and the de facto envoy to the Indians. Weiser was a German immigrant who had spent time in his youth living with the Mohawks. He spoke the language fluently, and, more important, understood and respected the land and the customs of its inhabitants.

When Weiser came upon the party, he spotted his old friend immediately, who stepped forward. Silent at first, they embraced and joked in Iroquois. Weiser and Canasatego had known each other for years as the principal spokesmen for their respective sides. It helped that each man spoke the language of the other—Weiser spoke Iroquois; Canasatego spoke English. Canasatego had asked Weiser to come sit at the council and had deemed him an honorary member, due to the fact that he had spent so much time with the Mohawks. Now approaching sixty, Canasatego was beginning to show signs of age, yet he still radiated wisdom and dignity from his tall, muscled frame.

Weiser welcomed his Indian friends. With Canasatego and Conrad Weiser in the lead, the head of the party walked the last mile into Lancaster, a rural farming outpost seventy miles west of bustling Philadelphia. Weiser had prepared a grand feast. Protocol required it. He had ordered a steer killed, purchased more than three hundred pounds of flour, a half dozen sheep, barrels of rum, and other provisions—all on the tab of the colonial government.

Weiser knew peace would not come cheaply. The Iroquois chiefs had grievances. English colonists were constantly expanding westward, past the Blue Ridge Mountains and into tribal hunting territories. The English commissioners brought 220 pounds sterling worth of goods to trade for a treaty: 200 shirts; 4 dozen blankets; 47 guns; 1,000 flints; 4 dozen harps; 202 bars of lead; and 2 half barrels of gunpowder.[10] The gifts also had a practical import. The Iroquois would need the arms to keep the French at bay.

By midafternoon they reached the center of Lancaster, just across the street from the courthouse. Weiser handed out tankards of rum to the Indian guests. Weiser was joined by his fellow colonial representatives. "To the health of the Six Nations," Weiser shouted out. A cheer erupted. The would-be diplomats left the Iroquois to set up their camp and rest after their long journey. There was much to discuss, but it was a Friday afternoon and they could begin the following Monday. What would transpire would arguably be the most important encounter between the colonists and the Indians since the first Thanksgiving.

Canasatego Addresses the Conference

The village greens near the courthouse were usually vacant, aside from the occasional grazing cow or roaming gang of local children. But for the previous two weeks the greens had been transformed into an Indian village. By July 4, 1744, dozens of wigwams stood in downtown Lancaster. Open campfires billowed. Animal skins blanketed the ground. The townspeople gawked from their windows. They had never before seen Indians up close. The more enterprising villagers in Lancaster traded wares among the wigwams. Gunpowder, shotguns, blankets, and rum were in high demand. In exchange, they bartered for furs.

But the real business at hand wasn't the exchange of beaver pelts for European goods. It was hard-fought points of diplomacy. In wigwams, representatives from both sides had parried back and forth for days. They sat cross-legged, the shade of the rushes and bark mats above giving some relief from the early summer heat. Tobacco smoke from pipes unfurled upward toward the small opening in the top of the wigwam. When the delegates weren't conducting negotiations in wigwams, they were discussing issues in the Lancaster courthouse across the street.

For the first ten days, the conversation had centered on the intrusions into Indian lands and the squatters who had settled on the eastern slopes of the Appalachian range. The governor of Maryland had been particularly obstinate. He had asserted that no Marylander had encroached on Indian territory. Canasatego rose to respond. He put the colonial official in his place.

"Brother, the Governor of Maryland," he began. "You went back to Old Times, and told us that you had been in Possession of the Province of Maryland for above one hundred Years." Then Canasatego parried: "But what is one hundred Years in comparison to the length of Time since our Claim began? Since we came out of this ground? For we must tell you that long before one hundred years our Ancestors came out of this very ground, and their children have remained here ever since."[11]

In no uncertain terms, he reminded the colonists of where they stood—on his land. "You came out of the ground in a country that lies beyond the Seas," he said. "[T]here you may have a just Claim, but here you must allow us to be your elder Brethren, and the lands to[o] belong[ed] to us before you knew anything of them."[12]

This was the eloquence that earned Canasatego favorable comparisons to the classical orators among the colonists who had read the great speeches of Cicero and Pericles. It was true, Canasatago had a soft spot for rum, but he never lost his facility for words; his speech became only more direct, and occasionally unflattering, when he was intoxicated.[13] According to Witham Marshe, a Maryland colonial official present at the conference, Canasatego carried off "all honors in oratory, logical argument, and adroit negotiation." Reflecting on Canasatego's rhetorical skills, Marshe later wrote that "Ye Indians seem superior to ye commissioners in point of sense and argument."[14]

Lieutenant Governor George Thomas of the Pennsylvania colony responded to Canasatego's charge that his people were in fact the "elder," more experienced people. "We are all subjects, as well as you, of the great King beyond the Water," he said. Canasatego, in the custom of his people, did not respond directly to the idea that he was a royal subject. He did not like to debate directly; he considered it rude. But Canasatego made clear that the Iroquois were a sovereign people, beholden to no one. And, indeed, proving his point, the French were just as eager to court Iroquois friendship as the British.

Canasatego's and the Iroquois' complaints about the squatters were met with vague assurances that the flow of settlers westward would be controlled. Precisely how that would happen was left unmentioned. The colonies lacked the armed forces to keep settlers from encroaching on Indian territory. But whenever possible, the colonial representatives redirected the conversation to the imperative of thwarting the French. Canasatego quietly nodded in agreement. If the governors would agree to keep their people from trespassing on Indian lands, the Iroquois would help the colonists against the French. By virtue of gathering so many different groups under the proto-Federalist principles of the Iroquois Confederacy, they were in a strong position to mount a united front.

A Printer Inspired

The knocks at the front door jolted Benjamin Franklin's head up from his ledgers. With ink-stained hands and a scuffed leather apron bearing the marks of a career in printing, Franklin ambled over to answer the door. He had been balancing the books of his business and welcomed a moment's distraction. In the nearly twenty years that he had lived in Philadelphia, Benjamin Franklin had built a modest empire for himself—though from looking at his bedraggled clothes, one would never know that he was among the wealthiest men in Philadelphia. Now, by August 1744, he had become a beloved author, once it was revealed that he was the mind behind the smashing success that was *Poor Richard's Almanack*, which combined Franklin's two favorite things: promoting virtue and making money. The bestselling book contained gems of wisdom and humor (many of which are still quoted today), like "God helps those who help themselves" and "Fish and visitors smell after three days." He published one of the most popular newspapers in the colonies, the *Pennsylvania Gazette*. Franklin had also become the colony's designated printer, responsible for paper currency and official documents.

Franklin opened the door. Standing there was his old friend Conrad Weiser. This was the kind of man Franklin loved most: unpretentious, with none of the airs or pomp of the hereditary aristocracy. He was one of the most knowledgeable white men in all of the colonies when it came to all things Indian, and thus Franklin found him and his vast store of Native knowledge fascinating. Franklin embraced Weiser and welcomed him in.

Weiser got straight to the point: "I have here in my possession one of the most interesting things a man could publish," he said, reaching into his coat. Franklin was tantalized—if Weiser, who had led such an adventurous life, called a manuscript "interesting," any printer would kill to get his hands on it. Weiser drew some papers from his pocket and explained: "The manuscript covers the most noteworthy treaty negotiations that have ever heretofore taken place in the Colonies."[15]

Franklin's excitement grew. He had heard of the recent negotiations in nearby Lancaster and had long been fascinated by the Native people who had inhabited the forests of America for millennia before Franklin's father arrived in the colonies. He asked Weiser what was so significant about the most recent round of meetings with the Iroquois. Weiser explained that they had at last made the commitment to the Anglo-Iroquois alliance that the colonies had been seeking for more than a decade.

Franklin took the sheaf of handwritten pages from his friend and walked to his desk to thumb through them. Franklin had become the most important publisher in Philadelphia by keeping an eye out for great stories, and as he turned the pages, he knew he held something of certain commercial worth.

Franklin's "Scheme for Uniting the Northern Colonies"

Benjamin Franklin had made certain that the words Canasatego had uttered at Lancaster—regarding a confederation of states and the imperative of the colonies' union—were immortalized in print and widely circulated after he received Weiser's report in 1744. And sure enough, the printed transcripts of the 1744 Lancaster Treaty became a commercial success, with curious colonists eager to learn what was on the minds of the Indians. Now, a decade later, Franklin was traveling to Albany, New York, to take part in further negotiations himself.

It was June 1754 and something was afoot. Franklin could sense it in the winds that carried news from around the other colonies. That news had traveled quickly. The governor of Virginia had dispatched a promising young army officer named George Washington to the Ohio valley. His mission was to deliver an ultimatum: the French were to vacate the area immediately and return to French Canada. They refused. Washington and his men subsequently raided French outposts and forts in the Ohio wilderness. The French were undeterred by Washington and the moves toward cementing an Anglo-Iroquois alliance that had begun in Lancaster a decade earlier. Indeed, their provocations in the Ohio valley were only growing. War seemed imminent.

Benjamin Franklin was more convinced than ever that the squabbling colonies needed to unite, especially now that they faced a war with France, one that could rage along the entire western frontier. Unification had been a pet project of Franklin's for years—

and an idea met with equal scorn by both London and the colonial legislatures. Why give power to some amorphous federal government? Suspicion abounded. In light of that suspicion, Franklin knew that any unification effort would have to unfold incrementally in a series of small steps. That might explain why he had created the American postal system and the American Philosophical Society— these were modest steps toward binding together the colonies and forging a shared identity.

The King's diplomats and advisers back in London were especially leery of any plot to unite the colonies. Divided, the colonies were easily manipulated. Nevertheless, London understood that the likelihood of war with France would make some kind of cooperation between the colonies necessary, and perhaps inevitable. It was with such cooperation in mind that Franklin had traveled up the Hudson valley on a sloop with "a pipe of the oldest and best Madeira wine to be got" to Albany, New York, to meet with delegates from each of the colonies.[16] They had two things to discuss: convincing representatives from the Iroquois confederation to reaffirm their allegiance to the English cause, and reaching agreement among themselves on how they could unify toward a common defense.

Franklin's interest in what he called "Indian Affairs" had also grown in the decade since he had published the transcripts he obtained from Conrad Weiser. He took special interest in Indian complaints about colonial traders fleecing and exploiting them by giving them alcohol. The situation got so bad that Canasatego's successor complained to the Pennsylvania commissioners:

Your traders now bring us scarce any Thing but Rum and Flour. They bring us little Powder and Lead, or other valuable Goods. The rum ruins us. We beg you would prevent its coming in such Quantities, by regulating the Traders. . . . We desire it be forbidden, and none sold in the Indian Country.... Those wicked Whiskey Sellers, when they have once got the Indians in Liquor, make them sell their very Clothes from their Backs.[17]

In 1753 Franklin had attended treaty negotiations in Carlisle, Pennsylvania, as a colonial commissioner. He was particularly disturbed by the scene that ensued after the conference: "They had made a great bonfire in the middle of the square. They were all drunk, men and women, quarrelling and fighting . . . [their] running after and beating one another with firebrands, accompanied by their horrid yellings, formed a scene the most resembling our ideas of hell that could well be imagined."[18] Franklin blamed the drunkenness on the greed of the white traders who eagerly sold rum to the Indians.

Franklin carried with him to Albany a pamphlet he had written, "Short Hints Towards a Scheme for Uniting the Northern Colonies." It sketched out what colonial cooperation could look like: a general council with delegates elected from each of the colonies and a colonial governor appointed by the King.[19] He eagerly shared it with his fellow commissioners in Albany, most of whom were skeptical of any plan for forming a union. After all, considering that they couldn't even agree to share the costs to build two modest western forts, how could they agree to form a confederation?

When the Iroquois delegation arrived at Albany, Canasatego was not among them. He had died four years earlier, in 1750. Tragically, it was likely his closeness with the British colonists that had led to his demise by placing him in the middle of Europe's colonial tug-of-war over North America. According to one contemporary account, Canasatego was assassinated "by Poison which was suspected to have been conveyed into his Victuals by some French emissaries . . . under the Disguise of Traders."[20] This treachery not only robbed the region of a great peacemaker, but threatened to tip the balance of power in favor of the French.

Chief Tiyanoga, of the Mohawks, who led the Iroquois delegation to Albany, was displeased. He felt the Iroquois confederation had been neglected and was not hesitant in letting the colonial representatives know it.

"When you neglect business, the French take advantage of it!" he declared. "Look at the French! They are men, they are fortifying everywhere." Then he twisted the knife: "But, we are ashamed to say it, you are all like women."[21]

Franklin moved to patch things up with a series of promises that included more consultation and laws that would restrict trade of rum to the Indians. Tiyanoga and the Iroquois were reassured and the alliance renewed, but if conflict broke out with the French, there was no clear understanding of who would come to aid the other.

Franklin's other major effort, his "Short Hints Towards a Scheme for Uniting the Northern Colonies," did not fare nearly as well. He outlined the federal concept—how each colony could benefit as part of a larger whole. A general government would be in charge of national defense and negotiations with Indians over westward expansion. Each colony would have complete control of what happened inside its own borders and have its own constitution. The commissioners were not convinced. They voted on July 10, 1754, and Franklin's plan was soundly defeated. As a conciliatory measure, they decided to send the plan to each colonial assembly and to Parliament in London for approval. Franklin would launch a public campaign arguing for union. In one exchange with the governor of Massachusetts, a staunch defender of the King's right to choose a colonial legislature instead of allowing lawmakers to be elected locally, Franklin hinted at the broader conflict to come: "It is supposed an undoubted right of Englishmen not to be taxed but by their own consent given through their representatives."[22]

In London and in the major cities of the colonies, the plan was rejected because it would have usurped too much from the King and his appointed colonial officials. Although Franklin was deflated, he was not willing to abandon the idea—at least not yet. Franklin would continue not only to believe in the need to unite, but also to work tirelessly toward that end.

The Iroquois Inspire Another "Confederation" Plan

It seemed to Benjamin Franklin that he had arrived back in the colonies from London just in the nick of time. Less than twenty-four hours after his return to Philadelphia in March 1775, he found himself appointed—by a unanimous vote of the Pennsylvania Assembly—as a state delegate to the Second Continental Congress. The following month, at Lexington and Concord in Massachusetts, a shooting war had broken out with Great Britain.

Of course, these changes had been brewing for quite some time. In 1765 the Stamp Act—which imposed yet another round of taxes on the colonies to pay for Britain's costly war debts incurred in conflicts with the French—had inflamed opinions almost universally in the colonies. In 1773 colonists had dressed as Iroquois warriors before sneaking aboard a British ship and dumping tea into Boston Harbor to protest the British East India Company's desire—facilitated by Parliament and the Crown—to control trade with the colonies. Increasingly, this led to talk of independence, and even war. Regardless, the colonies needed one another.

And now, working to ensure everyone stuck together at the Continental Congress, Franklin sensed an opportunity. It had been two decades since Franklin had presented his failed Albany Plan of Union. But the man who had used trial and error to pioneer so many inventions—from bifocals to the Franklin stove to the odometer—was not going to give up on his idea just because it had failed once. The warning of Canasatego to the colonists, which Franklin had distributed through the printing press years earlier (planting the seeds for his own Albany Plan) still echoed in his mind: "Whatever befalls you, do not fall out with one another."[23] Now a revolution was brewing—and it was important that the rebelling colonies act as one.

Franklin had taken the measure of the British government while serving as unofficial ambassador in London for the better part of the last two decades. His radical activities in pursuit of colonial unification and independence—including his biting satires and political cartoons that frequently lampooned the King—had eventually caught up with him, making him persona non grata in the British capital. Not only does that explain why Franklin had sailed back to the colonies in March 1775, but it also helps explain why, almost immediately upon his return, he was asked to represent Pennsylvania as a delegate to the Second Continental Congress. These were serious times for the colonies, and Pennsylvania needed someone who understood both the challenges facing the colonies and the current thinking in London. It is difficult to imagine anyone better qualified for the task at hand than Benjamin Franklin.

Franklin was not given to great speeches. In fact, he spoke very little on the floor of the Second Continental Congress. But behind the scenes he was persistent. In July 1775, he presented his "Articles of Confederation and Perpetual Union" to nearly every delegate. It was nearly a copy of his Albany Plan, giving broad powers to an assembly of lawmakers elected from each of the colonies, with seats allocated among the colonies according to population. Franklin also insisted on including provisions that would protect Indian interests by, among other things, providing for the mapping of Indian boundaries and the regulation of trade with Indians.[24]

Like the Albany Plan, these articles took their inspiration from the Iroquois Confederacy that Franklin had learned about from reading Canasatego's words so many years ago. Significantly, the articles were written with an eye toward forming a single, united country. Article I provided that "The Name of this Confederacy shall henceforth be the United Colonies of North America."[25]

Paying Tribute to the Birth of an Idea

Though the Continental Congress ultimately did not adopt Franklin's Articles of Confederation, they continued their important work of keeping the colonies united in the struggle for independence from Britain. Franklin's plan had been an important part of the discussion, supported by other delegates such as Thomas Jefferson. Certain elements of the plan would later emerge in the final Articles of Confederation adopted as the first national system of government in 1777.

While the plan Franklin presented was his own work, it envisioned a system that was unmistakably inspired by the Iroquois Nation. This debt was acknowledged in August 1775, when the Continental Congress appointed delegates to attend a special meeting with the Indians in Albany to inform them of the work the Congress was undertaking in Philadelphia to form a new nation.

The colonists had finally lit their own council fire, and they wanted the Iroquois to know who had inspired them to remain united, and to strike the delicate balance between giving the central government powers to wage war and manage the common interests of the colonies, while preserving the sovereignty and rights of the separate colonies that composed it. The colonial representatives addressed their indigenous neighbors with the intention of "rekindling the ancient council-fire, and renewing the covenant, and brightening up every link of the chain."[26] They reminded the Iroquois of "the advice that was given about thirty years ago, by your wise forefathers, in a great council which was held at Lancaster, in Pennsylvania, when Canasatego spoke to us, the white people, in these very words," words that had "sunk deep into" the hearts of the colonists.[27]

They announced that Canasatego's words had been passed down by their forefathers, who had proclaimed: "The Six Nations are a wise people, Let us hearken to them, and take their counsel, and teach our children to follow it."[28] And so they had.

Those who were busily crafting not the first, but merely the most recent attempt to unite different territories on American soil explained to those whose people had paved the way just how the Native traditions had been shown to them by their ancestors: "They have frequently taken a single arrow and said, Children, see how easily it is broken. Then they have taken and tied twelve arrows together with a strong string or cord and our strongest men could not break them. See, said they, this is what the Six Nations mean. Divided, a single man may destroy you; united, you are a match for the whole world."[29]

"Absolute Notions of Liberty"

There was nothing inevitable about thirteen separate colonies becoming a single, united nation. In fact, one generation before Thomas Jefferson put his pen to paper to declare independence from Great Britain in 1776, the idea of such a union was all but unthinkable.

For decades before the American Revolution and for at least thirteen years thereafter, the colonies squabbled with one another, in some ways just as they had with the British Crown. They clashed over territorial boundaries, taxes, and trade. Each colony had its own unique culture, defined by the ethnic and religious makeup of its inhabitants. In this respect, the colonies were essentially separate countries with distinct identities—not all that different from the patchwork of countries in, say, central Europe today. Puritan Massachusetts had relatively little in common with Catholic Maryland. The freewheeling, fiercely independent Rhode Island—a colony founded by dissidents banished from the Massachusetts Bay Colony—had little in common with the prim, proper, and, by the mid-eighteenth century, exceedingly wealthy Virginia.

But as the eighteenth century wore on, the colonies grew further apart from their European ancestors, and with the threat of war with France and unjust taxation from the British, the colonists began to recognize that they had common interests. Most of those who had settled in the New World were rebelling against the old, established order in some way. Some left the Old World to escape religious persecution. Some left to pursue economic ambitions, fully aware that for many, success would be far more attainable outside the stratified and class-conscious societies of Europe. And with each new generation of sons and daughters born on American soil, the connection to Europe grew more tenuous. The American colonies quickly became a radical—and wildly successful—experiment in alternatives to the European order.

Benjamin Franklin found such an alternative when he looked to his neighbors in the wilderness to the west. The Iroquois presided over a vast, powerful, and advanced civilization, and had developed and put into practice the basic ideas of federalism and political liberty without having any exposure to the European thinkers who suggested—much later—that such things were possible. As Cadwallader Colden, a colonial official with extensive experience dealing with the Iroquois, put it: "The Five Nations have such absolute

Notions of Liberty that they allow no kind of Superiority of one over another, and banish all Servitude from their Territories."[30] The Iroquois had a federal system in which five (and later six) different tribes maintained control over their own internal affairs but charged an overarching government with responsibilities of mutual interest such as common defense. In some ways, the Iroquois are forgotten cofounders of the magnificent American experiment.

The founders saw in Native American communities—including and especially the Iroquois—societies that were largely free of social stratification and oppression. They weren't utopias, to be sure, but for the Iroquois at least, there was a kind of egalitarianism, an informal democratic process, and a confederation that tied together different tribes in a permanent alliance. Native Americans like the Iroquois had never read John Locke or heard of the Roman Senate, but, nonetheless, they pioneered their own ideas of equality and the democratic process.

Yet Canasatego remains an enigma, unfairly denied his place in the pantheon of American founders even though, ironically, he was an American long before any of our Founding Fathers. Perhaps early Americans less wise and less worldly than Benjamin Franklin could not comprehend (or lacked the intellectual curiosity to consider) the idea of a Native people creating such a sophisticated system, so they simply chose to ignore it—much less admit to being inspired by it. Perhaps the Iroquois system gave too much autonomy to the individual tribes that comprised it, and those who preferred a strong central government—which was not the Iroquois way—did not want any Anti-Federalist rabble-rousers to get ideas from Canasatego and his fellow chiefs.

Canasatego was a great peacemaker, a diplomat who brought different cultures together by sharing a system of government grounded in common principles. His is an example that every American can treasure, regardless of personal politics. Yet his name has unjustly faded from history. That needs to change, especially considering that our drift from federalism has occurred more or less contemporaneously with Canasatego's decline from historical prominence; and because we have accumulated a $20 trillion national debt and created a federal regulatory system that costs the American economy $2 trillion each year, we have never needed federalism more than we do right now.

The third provision of Franklin's Iroquois-inspired Articles of Confederation of 1775 made clear the freedom granted to the individual colonies in the Union, explaining that "each Colony shall enjoy and retain as much as it may think fit of its own present Laws, Customs, Rights, Privileges, and peculiar Jurisdictions within its own Limits."[31] In 1777 the later Articles of Confederation ultimately adopted by the new nation made the same point in its second article: "Each state retains its sovereignty, freedom, and independence, and every power, jurisdiction, and right, which is not by this Confederation expressly delegated to the United States, in Congress assembled."[32] These articles were ultimately replaced by the Constitution a decade later, and while the Constitution gave the federal government considerably more power than the articles had, it still preserved the sovereign authority of each state.

James Madison, a staunch Federalist and a supporter of a strong national government, nonetheless understood the limits imposed on that government and the importance of state sovereignty. In *Federalist* number 45, published in January 1788, a few months after the Constitutional Convention, he explains the respective operating responsibilities of the federal state governments:

> The powers delegated by the proposed Constitution to the federal government, are few and defined. Those which are to

remain in the State governments are numerous and indefinite. The former will be exercised principally on external objects, as war, peace, negotiation, and foreign commerce; with which last the power of taxation will, for the most part, be connected. The powers reserved to the several States will extend to all the objects which, in the ordinary course of affairs, concern the lives, liberties, and properties of the people, and the internal order, improvement, and prosperity of the State.[33]

His language could hardly be plainer. The states are to have *more* powers than the federal government. According to Madison's explanation, moreover, the federal government was designed to concern itself with foreign policy almost exclusively, with nearly everything we would today consider domestic policy falling under the control of the states.

Federalist number 45 helped explain the founders' intent, but it was not itself law. Nevertheless, fewer than four years after Madison wrote those words, the basic concept articulated in *Federalist* number 45 was incorporated into the Constitution with the ratification of the Tenth Amendment in 1791. The Tenth Amendment made explicit what was implicit in the original text of the Constitution; it confirmed that the powers of the federal government are limited: "The Powers not delegated to the United States by the Constitution, nor prohibited by it to the States, are reserved to the States respectively, or to the people."

This view was generally accepted for decades, until political expediency got in the way in the twentieth century, dramatically undermining federalism. The story of how that happened could fill volumes, but it suffices to say that the Tenth Amendment (and with it federalism) is only as meaningful as the powers granted to Congress are limited. Under presidents, congresses, and Supreme Courts of every conceivable partisan combination, Congress has colluded with the White House to enact legislation that pushes the boundaries of federal power. And since the late 1930s, the Supreme Court has been largely unwilling to police the limits on congressional authority—essentially leaving Congress to police itself. "Hello, Mr. Fox. Here are the keys to the henhouse. Have fun!"

The American federal system is in peril. The founding generation would be horrified by the extent to which the federal government has taken power away from the people and moved it to Washington. We have neglected the words and lessons left behind by founding-era heroes like Canasatego, the visionary Iroquois leader whose service to his people introduced a budding American Republic to the principle of federalism—a principle that, when followed, protects freedom and promotes economic opportunity for all.

Critical to that protection, of course, is a clear understanding of the rights guaranteed to each individual. Unfortunately, as the new nation was gaining its footing, and even as the Constitution itself was being produced, that understanding was far from clear. A few courageous individuals helped bring the importance of individual rights into focus.

CHAPTER 5
The Bill of Rights: Elbridge Gerry's "Dangerous" Idea

THE ARTICLES OF CONFEDERATION OF 1777, WHICH WERE INSPIRED in part by Benjamin Franklin's Articles of 1775, which were in turn inspired by the Iroquois Confederacy, kept the newly independent states together during the Revolution against Great Britain and during the first years of nationhood. But it was an imperfect document, and the new nation's growing pains—foreign and domestic—soon required that they be adjusted. A convention called in Philadelphia in 1787 to undertake that work soon became—to the dismay of men like Luther Martin—a very different exercise.

Only seven of the delegates to that gathering, which became known as a Constitutional Convention, held the distinction of having also signed the Declaration of Independence in 1776. Of those seven, six would sign the final draft of the Constitution in Philadelphia. The single abstention among this group was that of Elbridge Gerry, a merchant from Marblehead, Massachusetts. Although Gerry was one of the most vocal delegates in Philadelphia, most Americans today have never heard of him.

The preamble to the Declaration of Independence, which Gerry signed in 1776, is the part best remembered by generations that followed. Nevertheless, most of the document consists of a list of grievances against King George III, who had, as the signers noted, "erected a multitude of new offices, and sent hither swarms of officers to harass our people."[1]

The declaration's complaints against the King remained fresh on the mind of Elbridge Gerry when he went to Philadelphia to attend the Constitutional Convention, and they prevented him from joining the vast majority of his fellow delegates in signing his name to their final document. Like Luther Martin, he was too skeptical of the plan to put his name to it, and his concerns fell along similar lines of those Mercy Otis Warren expressed about protections for individual rights. His primary objection: the new Constitution did not include a bill of rights that would protect individual freedoms from a tyrannical central government. Gerry didn't want the citizens to have any cause for enumerating another long list of grievances under the new republic.

Elbridge Gerry refused to trust that the Constitution in and of itself provided a safe haven for individual liberty—he was taking no chances when it came to the rights for which he had sacrificed a lifetime of service. His concerns, and the vociferousness with which he expressed them, did not always endear him to his colleagues in public services—but they could not help but admire his principles. Even John Adams called Gerry one of "the two most impartial men in America" (second only to himself, of course, as the account goes).[2]

The Reluctant Delegate

Elbridge Gerry was a slight man, thin, whose most notable feature was the hawk-like nose that dominated his face. His size was notable enough that, in 1776, as the men anxiously awaited their turn to sign the Declaration of Independence, a rotund Benjamin Harrison morbidly joked to Gerry, "I shall have a great advantage over you, Mr. Gerry, when we are all hung for what we are doing. From the size and weight of my body I shall die in a few minutes but from the lightness of your body you will dance in the air an hour or two before you are dead."[3]

His eyes often formed a squint when he burrowed down on a subject, which was frequently. And he was not shy about having his voice heard, though he was hardly a stentorian speaker. It was perhaps more than one acquaintance who described him as a "nervous, birdlike little person" with an unfortunate stammer he could never quite overcome.[4] Yet Elbridge Gerry was here in Philadelphia again, determined to make his case—and, undoubtedly, he irritated more than a few of his fellow delegates.

Twenty-four hours had not passed since his arrival to the convention, and Gerry returned to Mrs. Daley's boardinghouse exhausted. He could hear the convivial laughter of his fellow delegates downstairs, but that did not deter him from retreating to his room. Feeling drained, he turned instead to his one source of consolation: thoughts of his wife, Ann, twenty years his junior and expecting their first child (the Gerrys would eventually come to have ten children). Even as he made his way to his bed, a single, nagging thought consumed him: that he didn't really want to be at the convention.

Gerry, forty-three, had been reluctant to leave his wife and embark on yet another experiment in governing a young and divided nation. An early revolutionary, Gerry had weathered decades of deliberation regarding the young republic—and the memory of the British demagoguery paired with the recent upheaval of Shays' Rebellion made him extremely wary of tyranny—both that of the government and that of the mob. He understood the dangers of having too much power concentrated in one place. The hot, stifling Philadelphia summer of 1787 only exasperated his wariness. The "heavy, inelastic air," he wrote Ann, had given him a "Head-Ache" and "Loss of appetite."[5] Philadelphia's storied Quaker hospitality, or lack thereof, was more befitting of "Monks and Nuns cloistered in a monastery" than of cultured society.[6]

The son of a merchant, Gerry was a Harvard-educated businessman who had capitalized on his father's success and made his own name in international trade. He had amassed enough wealth to be considered a member of Massachusetts' "codfish aristocracy" and was a generous statesman who saw it as his duty to help finance the War for Independence, and later help pay down the debt accrued during the fighting.[7]

His civic-mindedness was hardly confined just to military and political matters. In one instance in 1773, when smallpox ravaged his hometown of Marblehead, Gerry built a hospital at his own expense.[8] As he grew older, however, his earnings dwindled—but he did not let monetary concerns stand in the way of his commitment to his country. Throughout his career, Gerry was respected for his integrity, declining to participate in government schemes that would give him an upper hand. He even supported Thomas Jefferson's export embargo in 1807, even though the action significantly diluted his own fortune.[9]

Gerry didn't want to advance an ideology. He didn't want to win points in debate. He wanted to get it right. This was his only aim and his only reason for traveling to the hot, depressing city in which he now found himself inconveniently confined.

"If Every Man Here Was a Gerry . . ."

When Gerry entered the hall on the second day of the Constitutional Convention, he couldn't help noticing the expressions of exasperation worn by men like James Madison and Nathaniel Gorham, another Massachusetts delegate and Federalist. With Gerry on board, any hope of a quick and cooperative process was now completely extinguished. Drawn-out deliberation would be the order of the day.

To many at the convention, Elbridge Gerry might have appeared as a bit of a show-off. Not that he didn't come by his erudition honestly. He had gone off to Harvard at the age of fourteen; studied the classics, ancient history, and political theory; and by the end of his studies wrote his thesis on whether "faithful subjects" could avoid the new "prohibitive duties" passed by the Crown—the Stamp Act—and argued that they could indeed.[10]

While the Gerry name was revered, it could also be feared by his government colleagues as a sort of death knell to any political expediency—thus, his company wasn't always welcomed by those with whom he disagreed. They knew he'd give them hell—and he never disappointed in that regard.

This was not the first time Gerry had served with Gorham, a man of Massachusetts who had succeeded John Hancock as president of the Continental Congress in 1779. That previous encounter with Gerry had not ended well: during the deliberations, Gerry raised an objection to a change in taxes on the states. He was denied the request for a recorded vote and argued that Congress's neglect of parliamentary procedure not only abandoned the rules to which they had promised to adhere, but also concealed from the public the actions of their representatives and risked impairing "that equal Representation in Congress, which is considered by the States so essential to their Liberties."[11] Gerry's criticism had hit its mark—Gorham himself had felt obligated to formally rebuke Congress after Gerry's outburst.[12] But Gerry wasn't satisfied and walked out of the Continental Congress in protest—not to return for three years.

Much to the undoubted dismay of those who supported a streamlined agenda, however, Gerry had no intention of abstaining from the Constitutional Convention, despite the personal sacrifices his attendance entailed. The task was too important; he firmly believed that "the fate of the Union will be decided in this Convention."[13] And he intended to apply every bit of the same scrutiny to the Philadelphia gathering as he had to the Congress of 1779, whether men like James Madison liked it or not.

Gerry was an anomaly to many of the men who traveled in similar social and political circles. The few he counted among his close friends, however—in particular John, Abigail, and Samuel Adams, and Mercy and James Warren—respected his principled (if sometimes paradoxical) stances, and found him to be a deep thinker and a loyal friend.[14] Refusing to subscribe to any rigid political dogma, he took positions that maddened those who believed a person was either a Federalist or an Anti-Federalist—and there could be nothing in between.

From the first, as he sat in a sweltering room with many of the colonies' finest men, the cantankerous Gerry expressed suspicion of nearly every idea being brought forward for discussion, from the lack of pensions for soldiers to the danger of standing armies; from the absence of a common currency to the failure to adequately protect individual liberties. And at every turn he asked variations of that pestering question: *What will this do to our freedom and our Republic?*

"If every Man here was a Gerry," John Adams remarked, with perhaps a mix of admiration and frustration, "the Liberties of America would be safe against the Gates of Earth and Hell."[15]

Of course, every man at the convention was *not* a Gerry, but the real Gerry seemed bound and determined to make up for that fact— right from the very first day.

An Early Deception

Today the stately Philadelphia structure we now call Independence Hall has a pristine aura about it—after all, it is the place where the delegates gathered to sign the two most definitive documents in our nation's history. The edifice didn't acquire its current name until 1824, when General Lafayette returned for a visit. But for the members stuffed into the hall throughout the summer in 1787, it seemed anything but free and pristine.

Gerry had come to Philadelphia willing to revise the then-in-effect system of government, the Articles of Confederation, though he was hardly naive about the grander ambitions of others—to gut the articles altogether. And it would not take long for one of his fellow delegates to provoke Gerry's suspicion.

Virginia governor Edmund Randolph, with the backing of James Madison and the rest of the Virginia delegation, proposed what would become known as the Virginia Plan: revisions to the Articles of Confederation to institute a "National Legislature," which Randolph argued was needed to curb the "prospect of anarchy."[16] Somewhat disingenuously in Gerry's view, Randolph insisted that his plan was *not* a departure from the articles, but a "remedy" to address their inadequacies. The Articles of Confederation left Congress essentially powerless either to raise revenue (making it impossible to maintain a military or to pay off the young nation's war debts) or to ensure the free flow of commerce between the states, putting an end to the interstate trade wars that were producing an unhealthy type of economic balkanization.

Gerry was sympathetic to that argument. Like nearly everyone else present, he understood the weaknesses of the Articles of Confederation. In an effort to protect the authority of the states, those who had drafted the articles had gone too far; they had created a central government that was nearly powerless. He was fully convinced that "to preserve the union, an efficient government was indispensably necessary."[17]

Still, Elbridge Gerry believed his mandate as a delegate was clear—he was present "for the sole and express purpose of revising the Articles of Confederation."[18] He objected to Randolph's plan to circumvent the articles not because he was unmoved by Randolph's arguments, but because a wholesale remaking of the government was not what the people of Massachusetts had sent Gerry to do. He also knew enough about math to realize that the few delegates who shared this view would vastly be outnumbered.

A Threat of "Civil War"

Once the intent of the delegates became clear, Gerry's concern was not so ardent as to be uncompromising. Indeed, if the nation's governing document were to be rewritten, he believed his participation would be vital to safeguarding the basic principles of republican government.

Throughout June he'd been battling one proposal after another, each of which he believed would have ceded too much power to a central government. He stopped an effort to allow the chief executive an absolute veto over any law he disfavored. And he pushed for frequent elections—to give the people as much of a voice as possible.[19] As adherents to the Virginia Plan continued to talk about a "national" government, he suggested a change in wording to something that seemed more in keeping with republican values—"the United States."[20]

But that did little to stop the tensions broiling between delegates representing the large states—who tended to favor the Virginia Plan—and those representing smaller states, who feared they'd be quashed by a strong federal government.

After the Virginians had made their case, mapping out a bicameral legislature with representation proportional to the population of each state, a large contingency of small-state delegates (spearheaded by William Paterson of New Jersey) erupted in outrage.

"How could we ever institute a system that disregarded the separate and distinct nature of the states?" they argued. Paterson and his allies devised their own proposal—the New Jersey Plan—which would have one legislature with one representative from each state. This state-centric plan would preserve the federal nature of the republic, ensuring that New Jersey, or any one of the small states, would be equally represented alongside larger states such as Virginia. The New Jersey Plan was more a modification of the Articles of Confederation than a total rewrite, which infuriated the Virginia Plan's advocates, who stood by their carefully laid intentions to gut the articles altogether.

The delegates, Gerry fretted, were acting more like petty bickerers than a "band of brothers, belonging to the same family."[21] He feared the outcome. "I am exceedingly distressed at the proceedings of the Convention," he noted, feeling that the divisions would "lay the foundation of a Civil War."[22]

With the convention at a standstill, the outspoken Gerry, who issued supportive words for both sides of the divide, soon found himself the chairman of a committee tasked with the impossible—reaching what would be called the "Great Compromise."

"A Foreign Sword Will Do the Work for Us"

The small group gathered before Gerry reflected a diverse mix of talent and stature among the delegates in Philadelphia. Among them were New York's Robert Yates (selected over his far more Federalist-minded fellow New Yorker Alexander Hamilton); Pennsylvania's stalwart, wily, and revered Benjamin Franklin; North Carolina's William Richardson Davie; South Carolina's former governor John Rutledge; and Virginia's George Mason, a patriot who shared Gerry's deep skepticism of a strong central government. There were eleven of them total, and they formed a committee chaired by Gerry that on July 2, 1787, was given the task of settling a question that had stymied the convention's proceedings: How should the states be represented in the new national legislature?

It's a "peculiar situation," Gerry noted while reflecting on the task ahead. But there was no alternative. "If we do not come to some agreement among ourselves," he remarked, "some foreign sword will probably do the work for us."[23]

Rather than endorse either a purely populist or strictly state-centric plan, Gerry and his fellow committee members constructed a middle path: there would be two legislative chambers. The first, the House of Representatives, would have its members chosen by direct election within each state, with seats apportioned based on population. In the second chamber, the Senate, each state would be represented by two senators chosen by their respective state legislatures. Thus, the House would be more responsive and immediately accountable to the people. The Senate, meanwhile, would preserve the role of the states as equals and guard against the "strong passion or momentary interest" of the people that could foist dangerous policies onto the whole nation—as had recently been on display during Shays' Rebellion.[24] To satisfy the concerns of men like George Mason, the Gerry committee put forward a provision mandating that any bill to create a new tax could emerge only from the popularly elected House of Representatives. This provision, the delegates understood, would protect the people (and the large states in particular) against the risk of "taxation without representation."

Gerry was convinced that the other element of compromise—counting enslaved African Americans as three-fifths of a person when counting a state's population (for purposes relevant to the apportionment of seats in the House of Representatives)—was nothing more than a Southern scheme for power. It utilized the very persons plantation owners treated as "horses and cattle" to bolster their own priorities.[25] But Gerry could find no alternative to keep the fragile alliance from shattering.

So the Great Compromise was born, and with it the hope that the convention would, in fact, produce a constitution. While Gerry had some reservations about the plan himself, he knew that some agreement was necessary to avoid a total failure. Still, the work of the committee did not satisfy everyone—especially not its chairman.

Disappointing the World

Reading the draft constitution that August, Gerry was amazed at what he found. It had been his idea for the committee to summarize all of the myriad proposals they had agreed to over the past months. Now that he saw the list before him, Gerry was concerned, and even fearful, about the monster they had created.[26]

Throughout the proceedings that summer, Gerry had spoken up 153 times—interceding on every occasion to defend the rights of individual citizens and to protect the distinct character of each state.[27] But after months of working as the moderator, months of reading and rereading the working drafts of the Constitution, something shifted inside Gerry. He could not shake the feeling that the draft product had veered far more toward centralized government, and far less toward respecting the people and the states.

For the next several weeks, Gerry worked to remedy his concerns about the Constitution.[28] He fought to speak through his stutter, and with all the conviction a person can possess. He called upon his fellow statesmen to guard against the perceived danger of a standing army in peacetime, which Gerry thought should be avoided altogether or capped at only three thousand troops.[29] He cautioned against constitutional language (later amended at his request) granting Congress exclusive lawmaking authority over federal landholdings within a state, "contend[ing] that this power might be made use of to enslave any particular State by buying up its territory, and that [federal land] would be a means of awing the State into an undue obedience to the Genl. Government."[30] He warned against creating the office of vice president, and putting the vice president in charge of the Senate, which he felt might give the executive branch too much influence over the legislature. "We might as well put the President himself at the head of the Legislature," he had argued on September 7. "The close intimacy that must subsist between the president and vice president makes it absolutely improper."[31] Some twenty-five years later, Gerry would serve in that very office under James Madison.

Most worrisome, in his view, was the fact that the new Constitution had too many vague terms about the rights of the people—terms that could be exploited by a future government determined to run roughshod over those rights. "Some of the powers of the legislature are ambiguous," he warned, "and other[s] indefinite and dangerous." He wanted the convention to succeed, for he knew that if it failed "we would not only disappoint America, but the rest of the world," and his list of concerns grew longer and more engrained.[32]

Then an idea hit him. There was one way that the delegates in Philadelphia might put his concerns at ease—one way to ensure that the rights of individuals would be protected. Why not put it in writing? That turned out to be his most nettlesome idea yet.

Gerry's "Dangerous" Idea

Alexander Hamilton scoffed at the proposal by the gentleman from Massachusetts. A bill of rights? Preposterous.

Gerry had made his motion on September 12, just five days before the convention would conclude. His motion—immediately seconded by George Mason—was to enumerate the individual freedoms that the Constitution would protect from government intrusion. The proposal was met first with silence, then consternation.

Hamilton was particularly unfriendly to the idea of a bill of rights. "Bills of rights are, in their origin, stipulations between kings and their subjects," he would write in *Federalist* number 84, a year after the convention.[33] He explained his view that because the American government was run by the people and not by a king, no such guarantees were necessary. He felt that since "the people surrender nothing; and as they retain everything they have no need of particular reservations." He quoted the preamble to the Constitution, which he found to be "a better recognition of popular rights than volumes of those aphorisms which make the principal figure in several of our State bills of rights and which would sound much better in a treatise of ethics than in a constitution of government."[34]

But Hamilton didn't just find a bill of rights unnecessary: "I go further and affirm that bills of rights . . . would even be dangerous."[35]

This was the view of most Federalists, and it showcases the differing opinions among the convention members. While men like Hamilton thought that the constitutional structure itself—the separation of powers, checks and balances, representative government, among others—would be enough to curtail any overly ambitious person, branch, or cabal, the Anti-Federalists feared that it still left the range of possibilities too wide for creative power-hungry types.

More to the point, most of the delegates, after debating for months, were exhausted. They didn't want to reopen old arguments while fighting over new ones. The proposal was unanimously rejected.[36]

When the convention dismissed the idea, it was the last straw for Elbridge Gerry. He could not sign on to a document that he felt could in any way endanger the people's fundamental freedoms.

"It was painful for me, on a subject of such national importance, to differ from the respectable members who signed the Constitution," he wrote to his fellow Massachusetts citizens, "but conceiving, as I did, that the liberties of America were not secured by the system, it was my duty to oppose it."[37] He warned as well about an "oppressive" judiciary; "ambiguous" and "dangerous" powers granted to the legislature; and inadequate "representation of the people."[38]

He disavowed the argument that the Constitution was destined for success simply because the convention had benefited from the input of the finest statesmen, including one who was by then the most respected man in the entire world: George Washington. "However respectable the members may be who signed the Constitution," Gerry reasoned, "it must be admitted that a free people are the proper guardians of their rights and liberties; that the greatest men may err, and that their errors are sometimes of the greatest magnitude."[39] As if channeling the same thought that would be penned months later by James Madison, Gerry was essentially observing that men—even "the greatest of men"—are not angels and should not be assumed to have angelic qualities.

Nevertheless, Gerry had not lost all faith. In his explanation for refusing to sign, he included hopeful caveats. First, he admitted that the document "in many respects" had "great merit" and by "proper amendments" could adequately preserve liberty. Second, he concluded that the "Union requires a better Constitution than the Confederation, so I shall think it my duty, as a citizen of Massachusetts, to support that which shall be finally adopted, sincerely hoping it will secure the liberty and happiness of America."[40] The republic could use the new Constitution as a base, Gerry hoped, and even-

Thomas Jefferson, though rightly considered a hero of liberty, gravely overstepped his executive powers as president in an attempt to write Aaron Burr—his own onetime vice president—out of history.

Aaron Burr, former vice president and presiding officer of the Senate, was accused by President Jefferson of treason, a capital offense. He was ultimately acquitted. Though hot-tempered, his skepticism towards the Federalist Party and its attempts to amass power in the central government has made our nation measurably safer.

Jefferson couldn't have Burr hanged, but he did manage to significantly reduce Burr's reputation. Today, history books recall only the man who shot Alexander Hamilton in 1804, not the courageous man who preserved the independence of the federal judiciary.

Luther Martin defended state's rights just as heroically as Patrick Henry; however, Martin is all but unknown today. His marathon two-day speech to the convention condemned slavery as "dishonorable to the American character." This "drunken, generous, slovenly, grand . . . genius" refused to sign the Constitution, believing it failed to protect individual rights.

Canasatego, the Cicero of the Iroquois, inspired Benjamin Franklin to understand the importance of a Federalist government that respects its constituents. "Whatever befalls you, do not fall out with one another," he famously warned. His legacy lives on, but he has been largely forgotten.

ILLUSTRATION BY JOHN KAHIONHES FADDEN.
COURTESY OF THE ARTIST.

JOIN, or DIE.

A transcript of Canasatego's speech reached the esteemed publisher Benjamin Franklin. The chief's ideas took root in Franklin's mind, and ultimately made him an active voice for the separation of powers and a confederate government. Inspired, Franklin created the most famous American political cartoon of all time, "Join, or Die."

ILLUSTRATION BY BENJAMIN FRANKLIN IN *THE PENNSYLVANIA GAZETTE*, MAY 9, 1754.
COURTESY OF THE LIBRARY OF CONGRESS PRINTS AND PHOTOGRAPHS DIVISION.

One of the most powerful and witty voices of her time, Mercy Otis Warren argued for a bill of rights to be added to the Constitution. Hindered in her political ambition because of her sex, she nonetheless corresponded with powerful founders, arguing in favor of liberty, and is indirectly responsible for many of our freedoms today.

The forgotten Elbridge Gerry fought for the Bill of Rights from within the Constitutional Convention. If it wasn't for Gerry's noble fight to speak over his stutter, many of the individual rights we unthinkingly enjoy today might have been blocked. Yet with a few strokes of Madison's editorial pen, Gerry's direct contributions to the Bill of Rights were obscured.

ILLUSTRATION BY J. B. LONGACRE.

COURTESY OF THE LIBRARY OF CONGRESS PRINTS AND PHOTOGRAPHS DIVISION.

Born a slave, Mum Bett overheard her owner discussing liberty with his guests and later wielded those words to make history.

ILLUSTRATION BY SUSAN ANNE LIVINGSTON RIDLEY SEDGWICK, 1811.

COURTESY OF THE COLLECTION OF THE MASSACHUSETTS HISTORICAL SOCIETY.

Mum Bett defended her sister from an attack by their owner's wife in the kitchen of their Sheffield, Massachusetts home. After that incident, Bett sued for freedom, arguing that the individual's rights outlined for all citizens in the new Massachusetts Constitution applied to her. She won, but her victory was soon forgotten, and it would be many years before her fellow slaves enjoyed the freedom they deserved.

COURTESY OF THE LIBRARY OF CONGRESS PRINTS AND PHOTOGRAPHS DIVISION.

One of America's most brilliant founders flamed out before his time. In 1761, before an angry British mob gave James Otis, Jr. brain damage, his electrifying legal argument casted doubt on the British practice of conducting warrantless searches. His arguments for protecting private property from government intrusion still ring true to this day.

George Mason's fingerprints are all over the Declaration of Independence, the Bill of Rights, and even the Universal Declaration of Human Rights passed by the United Nations more than 150 years later. He gave us radical concepts that overturned millennia of political thinking and centuries of political structures: a clarion call for freedom with an unabashed emphasis on the personal rights of every individual.

tually correct what he viewed as the mistakes of the convention. That, of course, is exactly what happened.

The Bill of Rights Is Born

"Are the gentlemen afraid to meet the public ear on this topic?" the representative from Massachusetts thundered.[41] It was 1789. Two years had elapsed since the Philadelphia convention, and Gerry was now a member of the first United States Congress, nominated to the post by friends—and against his own initial inclinations.

By now Gerry had turned more favorably toward the proposed Constitution, especially now that many states were clamoring for just what Gerry had called for back in Philadelphia: an express guarantee of individual rights.

The debates in Congress over the matter were occasionally boisterous. A bystander didn't have to listen closely for murmuring and moans among his colleagues—one could hear the objections loud and clear. Fisher Ames, a fellow member of the Massachusetts delegation and a staunch Federalist, vehemently rejected Gerry's idea that the whole Congress should consider every one of the amendments that had been proposed at each of the state ratifying conventions.

Gerry worried about transparency, and he wanted the public to have a full view of Congress's deliberations.

The objections to his proposal among his congressional colleagues left Gerry indignant. "Are the gentlemen afraid to meet the public ear on this topic? Do they wish to shut the gallery doors?"[42] Alas, a majority of his colleagues opted for a committee to discuss the matter instead.

Gerry had ideas of his own for appropriate amendments, some of which never made it past his impassioned pleas. He argued, for example, that the people should be granted the right to "instruct" their representatives on how to cast their votes in Congress.[43] Perhaps his most disappointing failure involved the proposal that eventually found success as the Tenth Amendment. The language read: "*The powers not delegated to the United States by the Constitution, nor prohibited by it to the States, are reserved to the States respectively, or to the people.*" Insisting on absolute clarity on the amendment's intent, Gerry pushed for adding a single word to the provision, to state that all powers not "*expressly*" delegated to the federal government remained at the hands of state leaders. The Federalist James Madison dropped "expressly" from the final version, an apt harbinger of the nationalized government that was already taking shape.

With the stroke of Madison's pen, Gerry was, in some way, written out of the Constitution's history. The version of the Tenth Amendment he fought for, which would have been even closer to the Federalist ideal and preserved greater autonomy for the states, was scrapped and a slightly weaker version used instead. But this one small word, Gerry knew, was of potentially great importance. And time would prove him right. Centuries later, the absence of this one word would assist Congress in arrogating to itself vast powers not enumerated in the Constitution, and thereby weakening the Tenth Amendment.

When considering the First Amendment, Gerry successfully advocated for a critical addition. He argued for the inclusion of "the freedom of assembly," which he considered an "essential right" to ensure the people were always free to organize and advocate effectively.

The Second Amendment, too, has Gerry's fingerprints on it. Ever concerned about a standing army clamping down on the right of the people, he successfully ensured that the amendment's first line read: "A well regulated Militia, being necessary to the security of a free State . . ."[44] As he opined: "When Governments mean to invade the rights and liberties of the people, they always attempt to destroy the militia, in order to raise an army upon their ruins."[45]

Gerry also introduced the motion to consider the Fourth Amendment—the protection against unreasonable searches and seizures—to protect Americans from an intrusive government.

It was an amendment that traced its roots back to colonial days and to the labors of lawyer James Otis.

Elbridge Gerry left Congress in 1793 after serving only two terms. His political career was far from over, but after his work to shepherd the Bill of Rights through the legislature and help forge the people's protective shield for which he had fought for so long, he could enjoy a significant measure of accomplishment.

The gentleman from Massachusetts proved prophetic in his conviction that the Constitution would not pass muster with the people without a bill of rights. Without the promise to move forward with a bill of rights in the first Congress, ratification would have proved elusive. His stance helped clear the path for the Constitution as we know it today—with the first ten amendments in place to protect a handful of particularly fundamental rights.

Gerry's inclination to stand squarely on his own principles would lead to apparent contradictions over the course of his political career. His contemporaries could not fully grasp the idea that he could support the national bank while standing in vehement opposition to a strong judiciary; or that he refused to sign the Constitution but later agreed to serve in the first Congress; or that after his clashes with Madison and his odd alliance with Alexander Hamilton on the national bank, he served as Madison's vice president.

But the common thread in Gerry's seemingly disparate actions was his devotion to republican ideals: preserving the character of the people and the good judgment of public leaders, protecting individuals from an encroaching government while ensuring that a federal system would guard against tyranny of the many or of the few, and establishing a nation revered by the world, but not dominated by it. And his principled stands, even if they ran against the grain, impressed many.

It is due in no small part to Gerry's insistence on a bill of rights that the first ten amendments were adopted in the first Congress, in which Gerry served. Thanks to Gerry, the rights enumerated in those amendments have for centuries remained protected from overzealous presidents and legislative meddlers alike.

A Fighter's Peaceful End

The carriage shook and rattled as it careened through the streets of Washington, scattering pedestrians and odd stray ducks and chickens, but the coachman didn't care. The man he carried, the vice president of the United States, was ill—and by all appearances, desperately so. Surely anyone who had his path impeded or his routine disturbed by this rushing through the crisp fall air would instantly forgive the intrusion, if only the person comprehended the gravity of the situation inside the coach.

At the moment, that situation was grim. Inside the jostling carriage, Vice President Elbridge Gerry was shaking and sweating despite the chill of the late November breeze that came in through the carriage windows as they sped toward his home. His breath came in strained, creaking wheezes. His mind, that instrument so finely tuned from years of government service to the nation he helped to create, seemed to come and go. One moment it was under his control, and the next moment it wasn't.

He could recall how normally that morning had begun: He had

awoken, dressed as he normally did, and set off for the Capitol to preside over the Senate as the duty of his office prescribed. On his way, he had stopped to pay a call on Joseph Nourse, the register of the Treasury, who had helped steward the finances of the new nation ever since the George Washington administration. But not long after arriving at the Nourse home, Vice President Gerry felt a strange tingling in his chest. Then he began to cough, and his breathing seemed to constrict. He apologized to Nourse, but the symptoms worsened. Nourse realized that something was wrong and helped the spluttering vice president outside to his carriage. The driver immediately set off for Gerry's home.

Gerry knew his home was near and he would soon be back in his own bed, but then, as he struggled to breathe, his mind began to reel. Faster than the carriage wheels could spin, his mind shot back across the plains of time. He saw his election to the vice presidency on James Madison's ticket in the election two years prior, in 1812. Before that, he saw his service as governor of Massachusetts as a triumph—one that had long eluded him. And even further back he saw his career as a diplomat begin and end with the mission to France that became known as the "XYZ Affair."

Finally, his mind's eye settled on that critical period in his career from 1787 to 1791—the sweltering summer in Philadelphia, the Constitution he refused to sign, and the amendments he supported to correct what he saw as critical flaws in the original document.

Gerry was no longer bumping along the quarter-mile journey back to his home and (he hoped) a doctor's care. He was back at the State House in Philadelphia, arguing for the rights of individual citizens to be put in writing—with the face of Alexander Hamilton, shot dead in a duel in 1804, sneering at him through the mists of time. Then he was back in his room at his boardinghouse, agonizing over the decision: to sign or not to sign the Constitution? This was his legacy, he knew, yet he stood aside—and his conscientious refusal became a legacy all its own.

Then he saw himself in the chamber of the first United States Congress, working to right the wrongs he had not been able to fix in Philadelphia. Now, through the amendment process, he saw his chance to make the Constitution the guarantor of freedom he hoped it could be. His legislative victories and defeats passed before his eyes: he fought for "freedom of assembly" in the First Amendment, and won; he fought for the rights of responsible armed citizens in the Second Amendment, and won; he fought for stricter separation of federal and state powers in the Tenth Amendment, and lost. All the way, he fought to keep the government small—including opposing the creation of the Treasury Department, whose business had taken him to Joseph Nourse that very day.

But had he done enough? That question plagued Gerry even as he struggled for every breath. As debate after debate danced before him—at the Constitutional Convention, in Congress—Gerry questioned whether he had done all he could for the cause of freedom, which he held so dear. The Bill of Rights, dismissed by his fellow delegates in Philadelphia, was accepted by his colleagues in the United States Congress, but many disturbing elements remained in the federal structure. There were, he thought uneasily—all his thoughts came uneasily now, as the carriage continued to sway—still far too many opportunities for the national government to reign supreme over its constituent states and their people. There might come a time, Gerry feared, when those powers would—in the hands of an executive filled with enough hubris or ideological fervor—be used to run roughshod over the very people whose rights they were designed to protect.

As the carriage finally clattered to a stop in front of Gerry's home at 1901 Pennsylvania Avenue, those thoughts of a fearful future began to slip from Gerry's mind. When the carriage stopped and the door opened, Gerry was carried out in a blur. His chest ached and every breath hurt. Somewhere, a disembodied voice was shouting, "Send for a doctor!" over and over, the words echoing down the decades so Gerry couldn't tell whether he was hearing them in 1814 or 1787.

No sooner had the vice president been carried inside and placed onto his bed than he "immediately expired without a Groan or a Struggle"—dead from a pulmonary hemorrhage.[46] The man who had so fiercely fought for the rights of his fellow Americans had ended his final struggle and arrived, at last, at peace.

Rufus King, who had attended the Constitutional Convention with Gerry and was then representing New York in the Senate, wrote immediately to John Adams when he heard the news: "Another of the Patriots of the Revolution is gone."[47]

CHAPTER 6
Mum Bett: The Slave Who Claimed Her Rights

W HEN WE THINK OF THE FOUNDERS OF OUR NATION, MOST AMER-
icans picture middle-aged or older white men. There is, of course, a
reason for this perception—there were no women among the delegates to the Constitutional Convention. Nor was there a single delegate of a race other than Caucasian. But notwithstanding the lack
of diversity among those in power in 1787, America was itself a
diverse nation, even in its early stages. There were other figures pivotal to the rise of the republic—including women and people of
color—and their embrace of revolutionary ideals helped to pave the
way for the open, pluralistic society we know today. Some were
outspoken women. Some were Native Americans who taught our
founders basic concepts about republican government. And some
were proud slaves who understood better than many of our founders
certain natural rights, including the right to be free. Though she was
born a slave, Mum Bett recognized the revolutionary fervor that
surged around her and understood that she, too, had the right to be
a part of it.[1]

Mum Bett heard those who gathered in her master's house
discussing the principles of freedom and liberty on which the new
nation was being founded, especially John Adams's words in the
Massachusetts Constitution of 1780, which proclaimed simply that

"all men are born free and equal." Even as a slave, Mum Bett, who had a strong sense of justice and integrity, knew those words were meant for her also. Faced with the cruelty of slavery, she took her master to court to gain her freedom the year after the Massachusetts Constitution was enacted to test the legal boundaries of what "free and equal" truly meant.

An "Irresistible Longing for Liberty"

"Where is your master? I must speak with him," the girl said in a quiet, rasping tone, without looking Mum Bett in the eye.

Mum Bett had been outside, working on the laundry when she first spotted the "smallish" figure coming down the Rannapo Road.[2] The apple blossoms were just beginning to bloom in the warm May sun along the Housatonic River. Bett had watched the girl turn off the road and onto the path toward the house, and knew immediately that something was wrong. The girl could not have been more than fifteen. It was not the first time a neighbor in trouble had come seeking help from Colonel John Ashley—not only a prominent citizen of the region, but, by that time, a judge as well.

John Ashley owned this house near the town of Sheffield in the Berkshires, on the river's western bank—it was a two-story affair built on a sturdy pine frame with a prominent chimney protruding from the middle of its gable roof, a combination of the Georgian and Federal architectural styles that typified the homes of prosperous early Americans.[3] Ashley also owned the woman named Bett. The son of an early Berkshires settler, Colonel Ashley had made, and was continuing to make, a considerable fortune by buying up and farming land, and operating mills and refineries around the area.

A 1730 graduate of Yale College, an attorney, and a veteran of the French and Indian War (his military rank came from his service as a colonel of the South Berkshire Regiment),[4] Ashley had thrown himself into the affairs of his community, serving on town committees in Sheffield, settling disputes, and presenting the town's issues to the colonial legislature in Boston. By 1761 he was serving as a judge on the local Court of Common Pleas.[5] As twentieth-century historian Robert J. Taylor would note: "Sheffield people scarcely did anything without Ashley's having a hand in it."[6]

Mum Bett, as one of Ashley's domestic slaves, had been attending to the laundry with her typical diligence when the bedraggled young girl stumbled upon the scene. An account written by someone who came to know Mum Bett quite well stated that she was known as a hard worker—"work was play to her," and "her power of execution was marvelous."[7] But the same account reveals that while Mum Bett appeared on the surface to be dedicated and resigned to her position as a slave, in truth "she felt servitude intolerable" and suffered under "the galling of the harness." In later life, Bett herself said: "Anytime, anytime while I was a slave, if one minute's freedom had been offered to me, and I had been told I must die at the end of that minute, I would have taken it—just to stand one minute on God's earth a free woman—I would."[8]

Mum Bett had, according to a friend, an "irresistible longing for liberty"—a longing that had been building over the course of her entire existence.[9] She would live most of her life in western Massachusetts and never go anywhere near Philadelphia during the Constitutional Convention. Yet as the winds of change fanned by the American Revolution swirled around her, she realized a simple truth that would take the rest of the country another century to understand.

The girl who showed up at the Ashley house that day lived in freedom under the law, but Bett could tell she was in a bind all the same. "I saw it was no common case," Mum Bett said later. As she looked at the fragile child, Bett noticed how pale she was, as if the blood had gone from her veins. Red and white splotches covered her face and neck, and she had bitten her lip to the point that it had begun to bleed. Bett could barely look the girl in the face—her tired eyelids hung low over her eyes. When she asked to speak to Colonel Ashley, Bett was struck by the hoarseness of her voice.[10] Bett had to explain that her master was gone.

"He's absent now, but he'll be home before night," Bett told the child.

"Then I must stay," said the girl, "for I must speak with him."

Mum Bett was a woman of action—it was "the law of her nature," according to her biographer.[11] She decided that she had to help this child, and immediately she took her hand and led her into the house. No sooner had she made the girl comfortable in a small side bedroom off the kitchen, than she heard quick, frantic footsteps approaching. Mrs. Ashley was coming.

Hannah Hogeboom Ashley was known throughout the town, in contrast to her generally kind husband, as a cruel and venal woman—especially toward her slaves, to whom she was "the most despotic of mistresses."[12] Mrs. Ashley had a "particular hatred" of young women who came to her home seeking her husband's help. As she stormed into the kitchen and saw Mum Bett and the unfortunate girl, her eyes, according to Bett, were "flashing like a cat's in the dark."

"What does that baggage want?" Mrs. Ashley demanded of Bett.

"To speak to master," Mum Bett replied calmly.

"What does she want to say to your master?" Mrs. Ashley asked, her voice rising.

Mum Bett responded in a calm tone once again: "I don't know, ma'am."

"*I* know," said Mrs. Ashley, and she flew into a rage. She heaped abuse on the girl cowering in the side room, screaming at her—"There was no foul name she didn't call the child," Mum Bett said later—and ordering her to get out of the house at once. All the girl could do was look up at the two women and make what seemed to Bett to be "a sharp sound" that "seemed to come right out of her heart; it was heart-breaking to hear it." That was when Mum Bett stepped in.

"Sit still, child," she said, looking at the girl.

Mrs. Ashley became nearly apoplectic.

"This is my house!" she exclaimed, and turning to the girl, ordered her once again to leave.

"Sit still, child," Mum Bett said once again. The girl stayed where she was.

"She shall go!" Mrs. Ashley declared.

Mum Bett said flatly: "No, she shan't." She looked into Mrs. Ashley's flushed face and continued: "If the girl has a complaint to make, she has a right to see the judge. That's lawful, and stands to reason besides." She knew that this girl—no matter how poor or downtrodden her background, or how dire her current situation—had a right to seek the protection of the law, and Mum Bett was going to help her get it.

Mrs. Ashley stared at her slave, but there was nothing she could do. Mum Bett, with her powerful sense of right and wrong, was a force to be reckoned with in the household, and even Mrs. Ashley knew it. As Bett herself put it: "Madam knew when I set my foot down, I kept it down." After unleashing a final torrent of abuse, Mrs. Ashley finally stalked off.

Mum Bett watched her leave with an impassive expression on her face. She had been dealing with Mrs. Ashley for years.

Mum Bett had been born into slavery sometime in the 1740s and was originally owned by Pieter Hogeboom of New York. The family lived very close to the Massachusetts border, and eventually Pieter's daughter Hannah Hogeboom married a man from the neighboring colony whom she had met when he visited her town on business— John Ashley.

John Ashley took Hannah back to the Berkshires and built the house near the Housatonic River for the family they would raise together. The house was soon filled with the Ashleys' four children: their son, John Jr., and daughters Jane, Mary, and Hannah. But they weren't alone. Also living on the property with them were their slaves. Though John Ashley owned only a few slaves, considering his massive holdings—certainly nowhere close to the number of slaves found on the plantations of the Southern colonies—the Ashleys, nonetheless, made use of enslaved African Americans to work in their house, tend their crops, operate their mills, and otherwise provide free labor for their various business operations. A 1771 tax survey listed Colonel John Ashley as owning five slaves, the most of any household in Sheffield.[13]

Among these slaves were two whom Ashley obtained from his father-in-law, Pieter Hogeboom: Bett and her sister Lizzie. Lizzie was markedly different from her sister, and was described by a contemporary of Bett's as "sickly" and "timid." Bett watched over her sister "as the lioness does over her cubs."[14] From the beginning, Mum Bett had a strong protective streak, which was informed by an even stronger sense of justice. Those qualities allowed her to stand up even to Mrs. Ashley when she saw someone who needed protecting— like the young girl who showed up at the Ashley home that day in May.

Later in the evening, Mum Bett tried to share some of her dinner with the girl, but she refused to eat, still stunned by the obvious trauma she had been through, as well as by the hostile reaction of Mrs. Ashley. As soon as Bett heard Colonel Ashley's horse approaching the house, she ran outside to meet him and to tell him about the girl before he had a chance to speak with his wife. Colonel Ashley recognized something was wrong and arranged for Bett to bring the girl to meet with him in his study after dinner. Before long, Mum Bett was holding a candle in each hand, lighting the way for the young girl as they climbed the darkened staircase toward the colonel's study on the second floor.

Colonel Ashley was seated at his desk, in a high-backed chair. The look of concern on the colonel's face was evident in the light the candles cast in the room. Mum Bett noticed that the girl "did not seem frightened," but her skin was still "all one dreadful waxy white." Colonel Ashley gestured to a chair, and the girl collapsed into it. After giving her name and swearing to tell the truth, she confessed her terrible story. It turned out she had been repeatedly sexually abused by her own father, and that she had finally escaped in the hope of getting help for her mother and younger brother, who were still in the cruel man's clutches. All the while, as she told her sad tale through her tears, Mum Bett was standing solidly behind her.

The girl's father was eventually apprehended, tried, convicted, and sentenced to death for his unspeakable crimes. The child who had wandered up the Ashleys' lane on that May day was given some small measure of justice. She was granted that because she was fortunate enough to run into Mum Bett, a woman who did not let her status as a slave influence her larger sense of right and wrong, and who wasn't afraid to stand up to a cruel and dictatorial mistress in order to see that an innocent person be granted the protection she deserved because, as she put it, that just "stands to reason."

Mum Bett may not have been trained in the law, but she recognized that this girl had certain natural rights, and she wasn't about to let a force for injustice like Mrs. Ashley prevent the child from having them. In time, Bett herself would face a similar challenge, one in which her choices would be infinitely more personal.

"Equal, Free, and Independent"

It was a bitterly cold Berkshires winter night outside, but the kitchen of the Ashley house was very warm, and the two enslaved women working there were glad for a few moments of comfort. Mum Bett (now about thirty years old) and her younger sister Lizzie were going about their tasks as quickly as they could. Bett was placing pewter mugs onto a tray, along with a jug of water, while Lizzie was removing a cast-iron pan of wheat cakes from the brick baking oven.

The dinner hour was long past. This simple food and drink was for the men upstairs in Colonel Ashley's study, who had been talking late into the night. They hadn't discussed much about their project, but Bett knew that the colonel had come back from the town meeting in Sheffield seeming more tense than usual.

But, then, tension was running high all around town these days. The increasing restrictions imposed by the British Crown were making everyday life tougher for His Majesty's subjects, and on her errands Bett had heard many grumblings that "something must be done." She gathered that, now, something *was* being done, and—like most important things happening in Sheffield—her master, Colonel John Ashley, was at the center of it.

Bett's intuition was correct. At the Sheffield town meeting on January 5, 1773, John Ashley had been placed in charge of a committee tasked with addressing "the grievances which Americans in general, and the inhabitants of this province in particular, labor under," and with preparing a report containing recommendations as to how the citizens of Sheffield should respond to such grievances.[15] The committee of eleven prominent citizens conducted its meetings in Colonel Ashley's study and was due to present its report at the next town meeting on January 12.

Lizzie went ahead to light the candles in the hall and in the stairwell, so that they would be able to see their way up the stairs to the study. While she was gone, Bett threw a shawl around her shoulders and pulled it tight—it was cold in the rest of the house. When Lizzie returned, she picked up the tray of wheat cakes, and Bett took the tray of mugs and the water jug. Carefully, they made their way out of the kitchen and into the hall, and began to climb the stairs to the second floor.

The house was quiet. Aside from the creaking of Bett's and Lizzie's footsteps on the stairs, the only sound was the low murmur of voices from behind the door of the colonel's study. As the women drew closer, the words became clearer.

"Viewing with the deepest sorrow the design of Great Britain," Bett heard as they ascended, "which is but too apparent to every virtuous lover of his country . . ."[16]

They were outside the study door now, and Bett heard the speaker say, "Deprive us of those invaluable rights and privileges," to which a number of voices responded, "Hear! Hear!"

At that point, Bett, balancing her tray carefully in one hand, knocked at the door. There was a brief silence, and then came a single word in Colonel Ashley's commanding voice: "Enter!"

Bett opened the door and saw the colonel seated behind his large desk, which was strewn with parchment, ink bottles, and quills. A few of his fellow committee members were huddled around the desk, while others sat or stood elsewhere in the spacious, pine-paneled room. It was well lit—many candles were burning, presumably so that the men could read the parchments they held in front of them. Several men were puffing at clay pipes. All of them looked up when Bett and Lizzie walked in the door.

There were eleven of them (Bett counted). She saw many familiar faces from around town: Dr. Lemuel Bernard, Deacon Silas Kellogg, and Major John Fellows among them. It seemed that before Bett and Lizzie entered, the men were looking toward one corner of the room where sat a young man, just slightly younger than Bett herself. She guessed it was he who had been reading aloud earlier.

"Ah, yes," said Colonel Ashley, gesturing at the women in the doorway. "Come in, Bett, Lizzie. I think we could all do with a bit of a repast." The men nodded their assent. Some stretched, and others relit their pipes or began to talk in twos and threes.

As Lizzie circulated with the tray of wheat cakes, Bett passed out mugs and filled them with water from the jug. Most of the men paid her little attention. But when she handed a mug of water to the young man in the corner who had previously been reading to the group, he looked her in the eye and smiled. "Thank you, Bett," he said.

"All right, gentlemen, we'd better get back to it," intoned Colonel Ashley from behind his desk. "That is, if our esteemed clerk has quenched his thirst!" Some of the others chuckled, and the young man who had smiled at Bett now grinned at his fellow committeemen and raised his mug. Bett and Lizzie took that as their cue to leave. As the women gathered up their trays and headed out the door, Colonel Ashley said, "Dispense with the preamble if you please, Mr. Sedgwick. Read the first resolutions again—what have we thus far?"

As she turned to shut the door, Mum Bett saw the friendly young man, Theodore Sedgwick, shuffle his papers. Just as she closed the door, Bett heard Sedgwick clear his throat. Lizzie turned to head downstairs, but Bett placed a hand on her arm. "Keep still," she whispered. The women stood just outside the door and listened, ever so quietly, to what they correctly perceived would be important words.

"Resolved," she heard the clerk read in a solemn, official tone of voice, "that mankind in a state of nature are equal, free, and independent of each other, and have a right to the undisturbed enjoyment of their lives, their liberty and property."[17]

"Equal, free, and independent." Those words were powerful to Mum Bett. And she knew exactly what "undisturbed enjoyment" of liberty would mean to her: freedom from bondage—not being owned by another person.

"Resolved," she heard Sedgwick continue, "that the great end of political society is to secure in a more effectual manner those rights and privileges wherewith God and nature have made us free."[18]

There was more appreciative murmuring here, and Bett nodded at Lizzie. They'd heard enough. They crept to the stairs and began to make their way down.

With every step, the words Bett had heard burned themselves deeper into her mind:

". . . equal, free, and independent . . ."

". . . a right to the undisturbed enjoyment of their lives, their liberty and property . . ."

". . . God and nature have made us free . . ."

For now, those were just words. But Mum Bett knew what they meant for her, and she would hold on to that meaning, nurturing it, until the day when she—like the colony in which she lived—could turn words into action.

"All Men Are Born Free and Equal, and Have Certain Natural, Essential, and Unalienable Rights . . ."

Since the Sheffield Declaration—the document drafted in the Ashley study—was unanimously approved in January 1773, the whirlwind of revolution had fully engulfed not only Sheffield, but the whole Berkshires region, all of Massachusetts, and the rest of the American colonies. In the run-up to the start of the Revolutionary War in 1775, Sheffield saw its fair share of rebellious activity. On July 6, 1774, sixty delegates from all over the Berkshires converged on the Red Lion Inn in Stockbridge to organize a boycott of British goods. The convention's chairman was Colonel John Ashley, and its clerk was Theodore Sedgwick.[19] The following month, fifteen hundred local men occupied the county courthouse in Great Barrington, preventing the session from going ahead—an event that prompted General Gage, the highest-ranking British officer in Massachusetts, to report to King George that "the popular rage is very high in Berkshire and makes its way rapidly to the East."[20]

According to town historian Lillian Preiss, while Sheffield was not the scene of any major fighting, the town contributed to the revolutionary cause by "furnishing men, material and moral support."[21] Sheffield men went off to fight elsewhere, and the town raised money to supply the patriot forces. At a town meeting on June 18, 1776, more than two weeks before the Declaration of Independence would be signed in Philadelphia, Sheffield residents voted their support for the Continental Congress then in session—even in the event its members decided to break away from Great Britain.[22] Sixteen days later, the Continental Congress—no doubt emboldened by expressions of support like those that came from the people of Sheffield—would declare the American colonies free and independent states, picking a colossal fight with what was then the world's greatest superpower. The most famous line of Jefferson's declaration echoed the wording of the first two resolved clauses of the Sheffield Declaration, adopted three years earlier:

> *Resolved, That mankind in a state of nature are equal, free, and independent of each other, and have a right to the undisturbed enjoyment of their lives, their liberty and property.*
>
> *Resolved, That the great end of political society is to secure in a more effectual manner those rights and privileges wherewith God and nature have made us free.*
>
> —SHEFFIELD DECLARATION, 1773

> *We hold these truths to be self-evident, that all men are created equal, that they are endowed by their Creator with certain unalienable Rights, that among these are Life, Liberty and the pursuit of Happiness.*
>
> —DECLARATION OF INDEPENDENCE, 1776

In 1780, in the midst of the fighting, another document was approved—one that was of great importance to Mum Bett, her neighbors in Sheffield, and everyone else in the former colony: the Constitution of the Commonwealth of Massachusetts, drafted by none other than John Adams. It was this document that Mum Bett overheard Colonel Ashley discussing with some of his associates at luncheon, after one of them had arrived with a copy straight from Boston. The men had finished their lunch and were poring over the parchment as Bett came into the dining room to collect the dishes.

"As you can see," one of the men said, indicating something to the colonel, "they begin right away with the Declaration of Rights."

"Indeed," muttered Colonel Ashley, who remained focused on the paper and began to read aloud: "Article One: All men are born free and equal, and have certain natural, essential, and unalienable rights; among which may be reckoned the right of enjoying and defending their lives and liberties; that of acquiring, possessing, and protecting property; in fine, that of seeking and obtaining their safety and happiness."[23]

He had just started in on Article Two when he looked up and noticed Mum Bett standing in the dining room doorway, her hands clasped in front of her. She looked attentive. Colonel Ashley surmised that she was simply paying attention to him and awaiting his orders.

"Perhaps some more wine for our guests, Bett," the colonel directed. Bett nodded and walked away.

Of course, she had not been simply awaiting Colonel Ashley's command. In fact, she had hardly been paying any attention to him at all. Instead, she had been concentrating on the words of that document, especially on the notion that "all men are born free and equal, and have certain natural, essential, and unalienable rights." They spoke directly to Mum Bett's own deep and abiding sense of justice—after all, if she, like everyone else, was "born free and equal," how could she be the slave of someone else?

* * *

"Thief! Thief!"

Tensions were rising in the Ashley kitchen. Breakfast had come and gone, and Mum Bett and Lizzie were taking advantage of some extra time to start baking the wheat cakes for lunch. But the fire was not cooperating. Lizzie was huddled at the brick oven, poking and moving coals around with a shovel. The wheat cakes were cooking, but there was a chance they might not be ready in time.

To make matters worse, Mrs. Ashley would periodically sweep through the kitchen, eyes flashing, to check on the women's work. She would stand over Lizzie at the fire, or over Bett as she cleared the tables, bark a few orders, and move along. As usual, they were trying their best to keep Mrs. Ashley happy.

At last, Lizzie was able to get the coals to heat up and the wheat cakes to finish cooking. She carefully took the cast-iron pan out of the fire and started removing the cakes. Bett, who was busy getting out the dishes, looked over and saw her sister scraping the pan for leftover bits of wheat cake—very carefully so as not to burn her hand. Bett could hardly blame Lizzie. The two of them had been laboring so hard all morning, they had hardly had the chance to eat anything themselves. Bett saw Lizzie take the scraps of wheat cake from the pan, roll them together in her hand, and slowly bring the small lump up to her lips.

"Thief!" The shriek cut through both women like a bolt of lightning. Neither of them had noticed Mrs. Ashley standing in the doorway.[24]

Lizzie crouched, frozen in fear, the tiny lump of wheat cake still in her hand, her mouth hanging open as Mrs. Ashley advanced toward her, so angry she couldn't bring herself to even shout. Bett knew what Lizzie had done—any of this food, even the scrapings, was for the family. In Mrs. Ashley's eyes, the women taking even the smallest bits amounted to stealing from their owners. As Mrs. Ashley passed the baking oven, she stopped and grabbed the closest thing at hand—the coal shovel, red hot from having been left in the coals. Now, as she came closer to Lizzie, she raised the shovel above her head, and Mum Bett realized in horror what was coming next.

It was a confrontation that would change Bett's life forever.

As Mrs. Ashley swung to bring the shovel down on Lizzie, Bett dived forward and placed herself in between her sister and her crazed mistress, with her arm above her head. Her arm caught the force of the blow, shielding Lizzie.[25] The pain was searing. Bett felt it start in her arm and immediately radiate outward, shocking her entire body. But she didn't scream.

Mrs. Ashley lurched backward, her eyes still wild. She dropped the coal shovel into the fire, turned, and stormed off.

"Oh, Bett!" Lizzie exclaimed as soon as their mistress was gone. Both women fought back tears as Lizzie helped clean the wound on Bett's arm and wrap it in a clean cloth. But a mere bandage on a physical wound would not be enough. Severe damage had been done not just to Mum Bett's body, but also to her human dignity. And she decided that she had been wounded for the last time.

"Won't the Law Give Me My Freedom?"

By most accounts, it was after the attack on Lizzie that Mum Bett left the Ashley home for good. She walked out the door, made her way to the road, and began the trek north toward Sheffield. She kept walking for more than an hour, going over what had happened and how it squared—or didn't square—with all the talk of rights and revolution she'd been hearing for the last several years. Bett did not stop until she reached the law offices of Theodore Sedgwick. She knocked on the door and was shown into Sedgwick's office.

The thirty-four-year-old attorney and the nearly forty-year-old slave woman were acquainted with each other. Sedgwick had been prominent in local affairs for some time, having helped with the drafting of the Sheffield Declaration (in Colonel Ashley's residence) nearly a decade earlier. Sedgwick's law practice was successful, and while he had taken time away to serve in the Revolutionary War, by 1781 he had embarked on the first steps of what would become a wildly successful political career. The year before, he had been elected to the legislature in Boston. He was also a close friend of John Ashley.[26] After some brief introductions, Mum Bett got straight to the point:

"Sir," she said, "I've come to see if I can claim my liberty under the law."

Sedgwick was taken somewhat aback. This was certainly different from the relatively routine cases that usually came his way.

"Well, Bett," he began, "might I ask where you came by an idea like that?"

"I keep hearing about all the rights we've all been given by nature and by God," Mum Bett explained, "and how all of us are born free and equal. The way I see it, Mr. Sedgwick, I am not a dumb beast but a citizen of this nation."[27] She drew herself up once again and asked: "Won't the law give me my freedom?"[28]

The wheels in Sedgwick's head were already beginning to turn. This could be an interesting case, provided he could find a strong legal basis for Bett's suit. He had a hunch about where to begin.

"Your ideas are sound, Bett," he said, sitting back in his chair. "But who taught them to you?"

"I taught myself," Bett answered drily.

"How?"

Bett allowed herself a small smile. "By keeping still and minding things," she said.

"I beg your pardon?"

"For instance," she explained patiently to the young lawyer, "when I was waiting at a table, I would hear the gentlemen talking over the Bill of Rights and the new Constitution of Massachusetts. In all they said, I never heard anything but that all people were born free and equal. I thought long about it, and I have decided I might try whether I did not come in among them."[29]

Sedgwick nodded his agreement. He and his newest client were of the same mind about the legal grounds for their case.

Mum Bett's Day in Court

The courthouse in Great Barrington, Massachusetts, the seat of Berkshire County, was not an impressive building. It was short— just one and a half stories tall—and squat, a mere 30 feet by 40 feet. It was constructed of plain, unpainted wood, and was, according to a local historian, "destitute of any architectural pretension or ornament, save a semi-circular window in its eastern gable and some little carved wood work about the front door." Standing in the center of town at the corner of Main and Castle Streets, the building was constructed so awkwardly that it jutted out into Main Street. Inside this "conspicuous object," in what was then described as an "ill-kept and untidy village," Mum Bett's case was to be heard on a hot August day in 1781.[30]

The case had been set in motion some months before, and in that time, several things had changed. For one, a co-plaintiff had been added to the suit along with Mum Bett: a man named Brom, another slave of the Ashley family. Unlike Bett, who belonged to Colonel John Ashley, Brom likely belonged to John Ashley Jr., who was now named in the suit along with his father. Brom may have been added to the case as a strategic legal move. Men, even enslaved men, still occupied a higher position than enslaved women in colonial society, and involving a man might have been seen by Mum Bett's lawyers as a better path to success.[31]

Other people had also become involved in the case as part of the expanding legal teams. On Mum Bett's—and now Brom's—side,

Theodore Sedgwick had procured the assistance of Tapping Reeve, a well-known attorney with a practice in Litchfield, Connecticut, some thirty-five miles south of Great Barrington. This was a coup for Sedgwick—Reeve has been described as "one of the most influential legal minds of his day."[32] He was renowned not just as a trial lawyer but also as a legal scholar and educator. In his student days at Princeton, Reeve had signed on as a tutor to two local orphans, a brother and sister whose father had once been president of Princeton: the Reverend Aaron Burr Sr.

One of Reeve's pupils, Aaron Burr Jr., would go on to lead the colorful career described earlier in this book. Aaron's sister, Sally Burr, eventually married Reeve and settled with him in Litchfield, where Reeve became known for training aspiring lawyers and eventually founded the first formal law school in the United States.[33]

Mum Bett and Brom had reason to be confident. After all, they had some of the best lawyers (from two different states, no less) on their side. But there was also considerable legal talent arrayed against them. An attorney himself, Colonel Ashley was not going to skimp when it came to his own representation in court. Representing the Ashleys were David Noble, who would later become a judge on this very court, and John Canfield, another Connecticut lawyer with a prominent practice in Sharon, not far from the Massachusetts border.[34]

The case began formally in May 1781, when Sedgwick and Reeve petitioned the Court of Common Pleas for a "writ of replevin"—an order requiring the return of illegally possessed personal property. In an application of a legal concept that seems both surreal and horrifying today, the "personal property" at issue consisted of two human beings: Bett and Brom. Through their attorneys, the two slaves were asking their owners to relinquish their claims of ownership. The court granted the writ, and directed the Berkshire sheriff:

"[T]hat justly and without delay you should cause to be replev-
ied Brom a Negro man of Sheffield in our said county Laborer, and
Bett a Negro Woman of Sheffield aforesaid Spinster; whom John
Ashley Esq. and John Ashley, Jr. Esq. both of Sheffield aforesaid
have taken and being so taken detain . . ."[35]

The Ashleys, however, refused to comply with the court's order.
The court reported that "the said John Ashley Esq. did not permit a
delivery of the aforesaid Brom & Bett to be made because he attested
the said Brom & Bett were his servants for life, thereby claiming a
right of servitude in the Persons of the said Brom & Bett."[36]

John Ashley asserted a legal right to own his fellow human
beings and would not give in after multiple attempts by the court to
fulfill the writ of replevin compelling him to give up his claim on
Bett and Brom. In response, the court decided to bring the matter
to trial.

Interestingly, the court was already willing to consider that the
two slaves might in fact be free and thus entitled to the same legal
rights as anyone else. Records proclaim the court "unwilling that
the said Brom if he be a Freeman and Bett if she be a Free Woman . . .
should be deprived of the Common law" by the Ashleys' actions.[37]
So the Ashleys were ordered to appear in court at Great Barrington.

That was where Theodore Sedgwick found himself that August
day, standing before a judge and jury and opposite the attorneys of
his old friend John Ashley. It is difficult to say what Sedgwick felt
about this prospect—whether he was at all conflicted about going
up in court against his friend. But whatever internal conflicts he
may have had obviously did not prevent him from taking Mum
Bett's case to begin with. Some historians, such as Arthur Zilversmit, have suggested that Bett and Brom's suit "was arranged as a
test for the constitutionality of slavery" in Massachusetts after the
new state constitution was adopted in 1780.[38] If Sedgwick was part

of an abolitionist legal experiment, then modern research by Harvard professor Henry Louis Gates Jr. reveals another twist to the story—before he took Mum Bett's case, Theodore Sedgwick had been a slaveholder himself.[39] Whatever the exact circumstances of how he came to be involved, Theodore Sedgwick was standing ready to argue Bett and Brom's case in the Great Barrington courthouse.

The Ashleys' attorneys, Noble and Canfield, began with a request that the case be "abated and dismissed," on the grounds that "the said Brom & Bett are & were at the time of Receiving the original Writ the legal Negro servants of him the said John Ashley during their lives," and that the Ashleys were "ready to verify" this.[40] This verification may have come in the form of a deed, title, or receipt stating that Brom and Bett were legally "owned" according to the standards of the time.

Sedgwick and Reeve were prepared for such a move and argued immediately against dismissing the case, asserting that Brom and Bett were not now—nor were they when the original writ of replevin was granted—"the Negro servants or servants of him aforesaid John Ashley during their lives."[41] That led to "a full hearing" of the case and "the evidence therein being produced."[42]

Unfortunately, the details of that evidence are scant. However, we can be reasonably certain that Sedgwick and Reeve argued for Bett's and Brom's freedoms on the basis of the individual rights outlined for all citizens in the new Massachusetts Constitution, which stated firmly that "all men are born free and equal, and have certain natural, essential, and unalienable rights."

Years later, a French nobleman, the Duke of Rochefoucauld-Liancourt, visited the United States and met Theodore Sedgwick. The two discussed the Mum Bett case, and Rochefoucauld-Liancourt gave a report of Sedgwick's argument in his memoirs. According to his recollection, Sedwick and Reeve argued "that no antecedent law had established slavery, and that the laws which seemed to suppose it were the offspring of error in the legislators, who had no authority to enact them. But in the crucial thrust of the case, they argued "that such laws, even if they had existed, were annulled by the new constitution" then in place in Massachusetts.[43]

One of Sedgwick's sons also backed up that position in an abolitionist lecture in 1831, in which he observed that his father's argument in the Mum Bett case hinged on "the practical application of the declaration in the Massachusetts Bill of Rights, that 'all men are born free and equal.'"[44] The historian Arthur Zilversmit, too, argues that Bett's attorneys "do not seem to have argued that there was a defect in Ashley's title to the services of Brom and Bett and therefore the implication is that they argued that under the new constitution no title to a slave could be held valid."[45] (Incidentally, Zilversmit knew something himself about struggling for freedom—when he was only six, his family was forced to flee his native Holland as Hitler's forces prepared to invade.)[46]

Jonathan Holcom, the jury foreman, and his fellow jurors considered the case. When they returned, they announced their finding "that the aforesaid Brom & Bett are not and were not at the time of the purchase of the original writ the legal Negro servants of him the said John Ashley during their life." They went on to "assess thirty shillings damages" to be paid by the Ashleys.[47]

Sedgwick and Reeve's argument based on the Massachusetts Constitution had worked. Not only had the jury concluded that Mum Bett and Brom were *not* the property of the Ashleys, but they had ordered the Ashleys to compensate their former slaves by paying damages. The court declared the jury's verdict "adjudged and determined," and imposed a further penalty on the Ashleys: the costs of the suit itself—another "five pounds fourteen shillings and four pence" of silver.[48]

Mum Bett was a free woman—or, at least, nearly free. The Ashleys appealed the decision, which meant it would be brought up before the state supreme court. The next time that court would visit Great Barrington—the judges traveled to the local courthouses in "circuits"—would be that fall, in October 1781.[49] For a few months, Mum Bett had the prospect of another trial hanging over her head—one that might reverse the lower court's ruling and return her to slavery.

As it turned out, she would be spared that ordeal. Ashley sent his attorney, John Canfield, to appear before the supreme court session and announce that his client had dropped his appeal. Canfield told the court that Ashley "confesses Judgment for thirty shillings damage and Cost of suit." By "confessing judgment," Zilversmit explains, Ashley had "assented to the lower court ruling that Brom and Bett were not slaves."[50] He had given up.

Ashley may have dropped his appeal—or been advised to do so by his attorneys—because of another Massachusetts Supreme Court decision, one rendered between the lower court's ruling in Mum Bett's case and the supreme court session in Great Barrington. In September 1781, the supreme court heard appellate arguments in several cases involving a slave named Quock Walker, who had been promised freedom by one master but later acquired by another, and had run away when the second master reneged on the promise of the first.

The Quock Walker cases were more legally complicated than Mum Bett's, but in their rulings the Massachusetts Supreme Court dealt another blow to the constitutionality of slavery in the state. Once the Walker rulings came down from the high court, Ashley and his attorneys likely guessed—and probably guessed correctly—that that same court would not rule in their favor in their appeal.[51] John Ashley decided not to go forward, and Mum Bett was free for good.

"Mum Bett" Becomes "Elizabeth Freeman"

When she first won her case (and with it her freedom), Sedgwick asked Bett what she wanted to do with the damages she'd been awarded. She responded in good humor: "Pay the lawyers handsomely!" she said. "And keep the rest until I want it."[52]

She had every reason to be in good spirits and was therefore inclined to be generous. Furthermore, she was genuinely grateful to Theodore Sedgwick, so much so that she went to work for him and his family as a domestic servant—a *paid* servant, of course. She started work under the new name she had taken upon gaining her liberty: Elizabeth Freeman. In the Sedgwick home she became, in the words of Sedgwick's daughter, Catherine Maria, "the main pillar of the household," helping to raise the Sedgwicks' ten children and caring for Theodore's wife, Pamela, who struggled with depression.[53]

Elizabeth Freeman formed a great bond with the Sedgwicks. One of Theodore's sons later recalled that he knew her "as familiarly as I knew either of my parents."[54] She defended their home from marauders associated with Shays' Rebellion in 1786–87, while the Sedgwicks themselves were away in hiding, on one occasion threatening would-be looters with a shovel.[55] According to another family story, in a different confrontation with Shays'-affiliated rebels, she brazenly dared them to open up her personal chest (in which she'd hidden the family silver) and shamed them until they "slunk away."[56]

It might seem as though Elizabeth—formerly known as Mum Bett—dedicated herself to the Sedgwicks out of gratitude for Theodore Sedgwick's giving her her freedom. But in reality, Theodore Sedgwick didn't "give" anything to Mum Bett. He merely helped her claim what natural and constitutional rights were properly hers, as an American and a citizen of Massachusetts. Mum Bett, like so many other Americans, was swept up in the fervor of the independence movement and did not let the color of her skin—or the fact that she was a slave—stop her from exercising the God-given rights she'd heard so much about.

She eventually left the service of the Sedgwicks and moved into a house she had purchased with wages she had saved. On December 28, 1829, Elizabeth Freeman died, at the estimated age of eighty-five—in her own home, a free woman. She is buried in the Sedgwick family plot.[57]

As Catherine Maria Sedgwick said of the woman who helped raise her: "Mum Bett had a clear and nice perception of justice, and a stern love of it. . . . Truth was her nature—the offspring of courage and loyalty."[58] These were the qualities that drove her to seek her freedom—courage, loyalty, and a fierce commitment to justice and truth.

Slavery may have hung on after Mum Bett's case, but she was a woman ahead of her time, and she exemplified a motivating factor in common with everyone who fought against the notion of a strong central government in the early days of the republic. It was the government, after all, that allowed the institution of slavery to exist. Mum Bett understood that this was inconsistent with the "natural rights" she had heard about, and she set out to challenge this unjust system. When she won, it was a victory for natural rights in the face of entrenched interests.

When the first U.S. Census was taken in 1790, nine years after Mum Bett's victory in court, her home state of Massachusetts was the only state in the new nation that was found to have no slaves among its population.[59]

Though Mum Bett is still honored and celebrated in Massachusetts, in the general sweep of America's revolutionary history—and the history of American slavery—she has remained largely obscure. When most Americans think of a slavery-related court case, it is usually *Dred Scott v. Sandford*'s shamefully pro-slavery decision of 1857 that comes to mind. But it is important to remember that decades earlier, amid the upheaval of revolution and independence, the Mum Bett case showed an early glimmer of the idea that the principles of individual freedom could—and must—be applied to *all* Americans.

CHAPTER 7

James Otis and the Trial That Gave Us the Fourth Amendment

Bᴇғᴏʀᴇ ᴇʟʙʀɪᴅɢᴇ ɢᴇʀʀʏ ᴍᴀᴅᴇ ʜɪѕ ɪᴍᴘᴀѕѕɪᴏɴᴇᴅ ᴘʟᴇᴀ ғᴏʀ ɪɴᴅɪ-vidual liberties at the Constitutional Convention, even before the American colonies declared their independence from Great Britain, the boundaries between government's prerogatives and our own rights had been simmering for a long while—and the debates are remarkably similar to those that continue today. The prospect of the federal government snooping on electronic communications or intercepting documents stored in a digital "cloud" would no doubt have seemed fantastical to even the sharpest eighteenth-century mind. Among those minds was that of James Otis, a Boston attorney and early American patriot who quite obviously had no understanding of e-mails or servers or metadata. Otis nonetheless understood the elegant, timeless simplicity of the understanding that would one day form the basis of the Fourth Amendment—the notion that a government must not violate the privacy and security of its citizens' "persons, houses, papers, and effects" without a proper warrant built on probable cause.

James Otis Jr. was one of barely sixteen thousand souls residing in Boston in the early 1760s when he began his fight against unwarrantable search and seizure. The Massachusetts capital wasn't just smaller than London or Paris, but also smaller than New Spain's capital, Mexico City. Though it had once been the largest city in the

American colonies, by 1740 Boston had fallen behind both Philadelphia and New York. Its population was continuing to dwindle, but what Boston lacked in size it made up for in patriotic zeal—of the proud, resourceful people who were simply pushed too far.

The city was in the grip of hard times. The Great Fire of March 1760 had destroyed 349 homes. The city's economy had stagnated. Bostonians were already thinly stretched, and the very last thing they needed was to be pushed around by politicians on the other side of an ocean.

Of course, that's exactly what happened. For years, the British Parliament had been busily working to ensure His Majesty's government in London took greater control over business and life in the American colonies. One of the ways they exerted their authority over the colonists was with a repressive legalistic cudgel called the "writs of assistance."

Writs of assistance faintly resembled the search warrants of today, but just barely. They gave British authorities unthinkable power over colonial property—all in the name of hoarding more money for the King's treasury.

We still debate today about the merits of free trade and fair trade, and the wisdom of slapping tariffs on foreign-made goods. In the British Empire of the late eighteenth century, the question was settled with an iron fist. Britain's North American colonies were to have nothing to do with free trade; instead, they were to be "protected" from foreign competition with British-made products. The colonists were simply a captive market to be exploited. In other words: *Buy British goods—or else.*

Not surprisingly, our colonial ancestors weren't too crazy about paying higher prices for the goods they needed, particularly if their own elected representatives had no say in the matter—which, of course, they did not. So up sprang a black market. Smuggling became a big business, especially in Boston—costing London huge amounts in lost revenues.

The British Exchequer wasn't going to take smuggling lying down—particularly from the upstart colonials. Lordly Britain would enforce its laws (even though the colonists themselves had never voted on them) and collect its revenues through whatever means it thought best.

Parliament got tough—in a kick-in-the-door sort of way. British customs agents pawed through warehouses, ships, private homes—and wherever else they wanted—hot on the trail of smuggled goods.

The writs of assistance allowed them to do it. They were official warrants, but these warrants didn't function like today's carefully limited warrants. They were deliberately flexible and open-ended. Think of them as operating in the way a dollar bill operates. A dollar is fungible. It can be spent *anywhere*. It can be spent by *anyone*. It can be spent on *anything*.

Now, imagine if modern search warrants worked the same way, and if the "bearer" (Britain's writs of assistance gave power to the bearer: they didn't have to be made out to anyone specifically) could simply barge in *anywhere*, looking for *anything*. Even worse, imagine if the bearer of one of these writs could compel others to assist him in his ransacking.

Here's the wording from one such writ, issued in Boston in December 1759: the bearer possessed the "power to enter . . . into any House Shop Warehouse Hostery *or other place whatsoever* . . . to make diligent search into any Trunk chest pack case truss *or any other parcel or package whatsoever* for any Goods Wares or Merchandize prohibited to be imported or exported or whereof the Customes or other Duties have not been paid, and the same to Seize. . . ."[1] (emphasis added).

That's bad enough, but it gets worse. British customs officers were further allowed to personally retain one-third of the proceeds of all the contraband they seized. Imagine if IRS agents could fill their pockets with a portion of your audits! They'd be digging up your backyard looking for buried gold or loading your new flat-screen TV onto their SUV.[2] Or, more likely, they'd be forcing the local sheriff or your next-door neighbor to do the digging.

There was, however, one limitation on these extremely obnoxious pieces of parchment: they expired when the King "expired"—they were good only during the reign of the monarch in whose name they were issued. But waiting for this expiration could take a while—a good long while. Kings weren't exactly term limited.

That was one of many reasons October 25, 1760, was such a significant date. Britain's seventy-six-year-old, German-born King George II finally died, which meant that any existing writ had to be reissued.[3]

The bad news: Britain's new monarch, King George III, was just twenty-two years old—any writs he might issue would remain in force for a very long time. His expected longevity could add up to a lot of rummaging through private property.

The Making of a Champion of Liberty

James Otis (that's what people invariably called James Otis Jr., while his father was always "Colonel Otis") was already a budding intellectual when British overstepping began to get out of hand. He had entered Harvard in 1739 at the tender age of fourteen. He wasn't quite sure of what he wanted to do upon his graduation in 1743, so he took a few years off to clear his mind before deciding to pursue a career in law.

As it turned out, entering the legal profession was a good choice for James Otis. His career quickly blossomed. He relocated his practice from Plymouth to Boston in 1750. He soon found himself taking cases far and wide, even traveling to Rhode Island and to far-off Halifax, Nova Scotia, where he defended three men accused of piracy. His marriage in 1755 to the beautiful but shy Ruth Cunningham, daughter of the wealthy merchant Nathaniel Cunningham, only cemented his social and financial position. In those years he took little interest in the politics of the colony.

In 1760 he published a seventy-two-page volume, entitled *The rudiments of Latin prosody: with, a dissertation on letters, and the principles of harmony, in poetic and prosaic composition*.[4] He also wrote but never published a companion volume on Greek prosody, but as he ruefully observed, "There were no Greek types in the country, or, if there were, no printer knew how to set them."[5]

Yes, he was an intellectual—at Harvard his interests were classical and literary—but also a bit of an eccentric. Once he played his violin for a few friends. Suddenly, in the middle of the recital, he stopped and exclaimed, "So Orpheus fiddled, and so danced the brutes!"[6] With that he dropped his instrument and fled into the garden—and never played again.

Eccentric as he was, he was also a friend of freedom and was well regarded. John Adams later wrote: "There was not a citizen of Boston more universally beloved for his learning, ingenuity, every domestic and social virtue, and conscientious conduct in every relation of life."[7]

Considerably less friendly to freedom was the man who became the chief judge of the Massachusetts Superior Court of Judicature in 1760. Appointed in 1760, Thomas Hutchinson ("tall, slender, fair-complexioned, and fair spoken")[8] was intelligent and quite respected—"a very good gentleman, who captivated half the pretty ladies in the colony [and] more than half the gentlemen."[9]

Captivating though he was, Hutchinson showed signs of serious corruption. He was already lieutenant governor *and* the Suffolk County probate judge *and* a member of the governor's council. His brother held another judgeship. Public service is admirable, but having the same person hold so many public offices at the same time can cause problems.

Also raising eyebrows was Hutchinson's own lack of qualifications for these various posts. Although two of Hutchinson's jobs were judgeships, Hutchinson was not even trained as a lawyer. Hutchinson's lack of legal expertise must have frustrated members of the Massachusetts bar. It certainly angered one in particular: Colonel James Otis of Barnstable, the father of James Otis Jr. Not one but two former colonial governors had promised Colonel Otis of Barnstable a supreme court seat. But when a seat finally came open, the sitting governor, Sir Francis Bernard, gave it instead to Hutchinson. Making matters worse was the enmity between the two men—Hutchinson had denigrated Colonel Otis's character, and Otis knew about it.[10] Colonel Otis was incensed.

Equally livid—perhaps even more so—was his son. Governor Bernard's appointment of Thomas Hutchinson enraged the younger James Otis. "Upon the Governor's nominating me to office," Hutchinson would later write, "one of the Gentleman's sons who was solicitous for it swore revenge,"[11] claiming that the younger Otis vowed to "set the province in flames, if he perished by the fires."[12]

James Otis Jr. may have held a personal grudge against Hutchinson, but that was soon overtaken by the rage he felt on behalf of all free men and women of Boston.

"From So Small a Spark, a Great Fire"

The critical case that would pit James Otis against Thomas Hutchinson—and liberty against tyranny—was initiated by a man named James Cockle. A new collector of customs, Cockle (a fellow in need of cash—and whatever else he could net from seizing smuggled goods) had arrived in Massachusetts from England in 1760[13] and quickly applied for a writ of assistance to aid him in his duties. The court, however, did not grant his request right away, and sixty-three merchants opposed to the writs petitioned the five-member Massachusetts Superior Court of Judicature (Thomas Hutchinson's new court) to "be heard by themselves and counsel upon the Subject of the Writs of Assistance."[14]

The Otis family may have been on the outs with Hutchinson, but it still commanded a good bit of influence in provincial politics. Young James now served as advocate general, or chief prosecutor, of the Massachusetts Vice-Admiralty Court. In that capacity, James would have to oppose these sixty-three merchants in their suit for liberty. He would have been a formidable opponent. Otis's "reputation as a scholar, a lawyer, a reasoner, and a man of spirit, was then very high," recalled John Adams. A fellow attorney, James Putnam, told Adams that "Otis was by far the most able, manly, and commanding character of his age at the bar."[15]

However, "the man of spirit" decided in this case that his spirit directed him away from the duties of his position. James Otis shocked just about everyone by refusing to defend Cockle's writ request.

Not only did he refuse, he resigned his lucrative and prestigious position as advocate general, agreed to take the merchants' case, and waived any payment for his services. "In such a cause," he proclaimed, "I despise all fees."[16]

Thomas Hutchinson bitterly speculated that Otis's actions could be attributed solely to James's father not having received his promised judgeship. "From so small a spark," Hutchinson later wrote, "a great fire seems to have been kindled."[17]

But even if James Otis was pleased to take on the man who had wronged his father, simple revenge cannot have been his primary motive for resigning his prosecutor position, seemingly upending his entire career. Something deeper was driving him. "Who shall say that James Otis's subsequent resistance to tyranny was not the outcome of patriotism, and patriotism alone?" asked one chronicler of the Otis family's history, "Only those who would tear up lilies and plant nettles in their place."[18]

Under the Gaze of Kings

On the morning the legal battle against the writs began, thirty-five-year-old James Otis adjusted his wig and prepared his mind to marshal his arguments for the case ahead. As he stood at the bench, the eyes of British rulers (past and present) bore down on him. Arrayed before him on their bench at the Council Chamber in Boston's Old Town House on that day—February 25, 1761—were the judges of the Massachusetts Supreme Court who, resplendent in their elegant attire of "voluminous wigs, broad bands, and robes of scarlet cloth,"[19] represented the reigning King George III. Towering over the day's proceedings were two huge portraits of two of Britain's late kings, Charles II and James II. Neither monarch was a particular friend of liberty, and James II (Britain's last Catholic king) had even been deposed in the Glorious Revolution of 1688. Governor Bernard had just recently refurbished and rehung these portraits—quite surely as a studied affront and point-blank warning to the current king's fractious subjects, whom Bernard was charged to keep in line.

This great room tingled with excitement, crowded not only by scores of litigants but also by those who had come merely to observe this legal battle royal. Among the latter was twenty-six-year-old attorney John Adams, admitted to the bar in 1758, who now joined the crowd bewigged and clad in a black barrister's gown,[20] looking very much, he conceded many years later, "like a short, thick archbishop of Canterbury."[21] It had long been his habit to carefully record his daily events in a diary, and today would be no exception. It is thanks to Adams's recollections that we know much of what transpired on that gloomy February day.

Standing in defense of these writs was Otis's onetime mentor, Jeremiah Gridley. The fifty-nine-year-old Gridley was one of the province's premier attorneys, and he had helped to train Otis as a lawyer (in that period, one became a lawyer by serving as an apprentice; formal law schools were not yet commonplace). He had replaced Otis as advocate general after his resignation to take the merchants' case against the writs, and his experience and skill would make him a formidable adversary.[22]

"Gridley's Grandeur consists in his great Learning," John Adams noted, "his great Parts and his majestic Manner. . . . Gridley has a bold, spirited Manner of Speaking, but is too stiff, has too little Command of the Muscles of his face. His Words seem to pierce and search, have something quick and animating. He is a great Reasoner, and has a very vivid Imagination."[23]

It did not, however, require much imagination at all for Gridley to make his case. When he stood to present his side, his argument seemed to be the easier one. In the British system, Parliament could pretty much do as it pleased. And if the people suffered—well, that was just too bad. "The necessity of having public taxes effectually and speedily collected," Gridley argued, "is of infinitely greater moment to the whole, than the Liberty of any Individual."[24]

Before Otis himself stood to respond, it fell to his co-counsel, forty-nine-year-old Oxenbridge Thacher, to first counter Gridley's arguments. He, too, had studied with Gridley. A Harvard valedictorian, Thacher had originally aimed at the ministry, but a weak speaking voice derailed that ambition.[25]

Thacher's argument was purely legalistic. He pointed out that when Parliament had initiated the power of the Exchequer to issue writs of assistance in 1662 (and in 1696 had allowed customs officials in the American colonies to apply for such writs), it had never delegated to the Massachusetts Superior Court the right to issue such writs, as James Cockle had requested.

"What little there was to say was well said by Oxenbridge Thacher,"[26] John Adams noted; Thacher's "softness of manners, . . . ingenuity, and cool reasoning"[27] were on full display. Thacher had done his best for what he could probably tell was essentially a lost cause.

It was up to Otis to dispense with the technicalities on which Thacher had relied and to tie the case to wider issues. In doing so, he was determined to be neither soft, nor cool, nor amiable.

He planned to set the world ablaze.

He rose at two in the afternoon and bombarded his opponents for a full four and a half hours, well past dusk, his features eventually illuminated only by flickering candlelight. "It was," said Adams "a moral spectacle more affecting to me than any I have ever since seen upon the stage, to observe a pupil [Otis] treating his master [Gridley] with all the deference, respect, esteem and affection of a son to a father, and that without the least affectation; while he baffled and confounded all his authorities, confuted all his arguments, and reduced him to silence!"[28]

Otis attacked on all fronts.

He tied the case to traditional British rights, dating back to the ancient Saxon law and to Runnymede and to King John I's Magna Carta. He thundered that "[t]axation without representation is tyranny"[29] and vowed that "I will to my dying day . . . oppose all such instruments of slavery on the one hand or villany on the other as this writ of assistance is . . . No acts of parliament can establish such a writ; tho it would be in the very words of the petition 'twould be void. An act against the constitution is void."[30]

His mention of "the constitution" is especially interesting. James Otis was declaring that any act going against a constitution (even Britain's, which was more of a loose collection of legal precedents) was null and not to be obeyed.

He preached an open resistance not only to the writs of assistance but also to Britain's entire high-handed treatment of its colonies: "[I]f the King of Great Britain in person were encamped on Boston Common, at the head of twenty thousand men, with all his navy on our coast," Otis taunted the royal authorities before him, "he would not be able to execute these laws."[31]

Otis, John Adams admiringly continued, "displayed so comprehensive a knowledge of the subject, showed not only the illegality of the writ, its insidious and mischievous tendency, but he laid open the views and designs of Great Britain, in taxing us, of destroying our charters and assuming the powers of our government, legislative, executive, and judicial, external and internal, civil and ecclesiastical, temporal and spiritual; and all this was performed with such a profusion of learning, such convincing argument, and such a torrent of sublime and pathetic eloquence, that a great crowd of spectators and auditors went away absolutely electrified."[32]

Electrified, indeed. All arguments in court are necessarily predicated on law—generally a combination of statute and precedent. Some arguments, however, also find support (at least implicitly) in a higher law—a grander, eternal law. The words comprising such arguments flow not only from musty legal texts, but also from the sentiments that dwell within the heart of every person who longs for liberty, freedom, and, in the words of the Bible and of George Washington, for the right to sit safely "under their vine and fig tree."

James Otis framed his argument around four key objections to the writs. "In the first place," he began, "the writ is universal, being directed 'to all and singular justices, sheriffs, constables, and all other officers and subjects'; so that, in short, it is directed to every subject in the King's dominions." In Otis's mind, this meant "every one with this writ may be a tyrant; if this commission be legal, a tyrant in a legal manner, also, may control, imprison, or murder any one within the realm"—hardly a picture of a just society.

Otis continued: "In the next place, it is perpetual; there is no return. A man is accountable to no person for his doings." Homing in on the danger of individual misuse of these writs, Otis charged that "every man may reign secure in his petty tyranny, and spread terror and desolation around him, until the trump of the Archangel shall excite different emotions in his soul."

"In the third place," Otis argued, "a person with this writ, in the daytime, may enter all houses, shops, etc., at will, and command all to assist him." Finally, he concluded: "Fourthly, by this writ not only deputies, etc., but even their menial servants, are allowed to lord it over us. What is this but to have the curse of Canaan with a witness on us: to be the servants of servants, the most despicable of God's creation?"

Then he drove his point home: "Now, one of the most essential branches of English liberty is the freedom of one's house. A man's house is his castle; and whilst he is quiet, he is as well guarded as a prince in his castle." But our individual principalities were in danger. "This writ, if it should be declared legal," according to Otis, "would totally annihilate this privilege."

"Custom-house officers may enter our houses when they please," he thundered. "We are commanded to permit their entry. Their menial servants may enter, may break locks, bars, and everything in their way; and whether they break through malice or revenge, no man, no court can inquire. Bare suspicion without oath is sufficient."[33]

"Otis was a flame of fire!" Adams exclaimed, "with a promptitude of classical allusions, a depth of research, a rapid summary of historical events and dates, a profusion of legal authorities, prophetic glance of his eyes into futurity, and a rapid torrent of impetuous eloquence."[34]

While much of the "established" law was clearly on the Crown's side, the white-hot force of Otis's passion and moral certainty had just as clearly framed this case in a new light. Absent Otis's argument, Hutchinson and his four associate justices would have predictably ruled in favor of Customs Collector Cockle. Now, however, all bets were off; Otis had effectively altered the legal and political landscape. Hutchinson punted, urging his four fellow jurists to "continue the question until next term [and] to write to England for information concerning the subject."[35]

Months passed before Hutchinson received his reply. It was a disappointment when it came. In November 1761, London advised him to affirm Cockle's writ of assistance. Hutchinson dutifully complied.[36] He even soon issued a new writ, this time to the "Surveyor and Searcher" of the port of Boston, Charles Paxton.[37] Nevertheless, authorities were now at least a little more hesitant to enforce these widely despised instruments of royal power.

James Otis had officially lost the battle. But even if he did not realize it at the time, he had won the war—not only concerning these writs but also about the very nature of the colonies' relationship to their mother country. "Then and there," summarized John Adams, "was the first scene of the first act of opposition to the arbitrary claims of Great Britain. Then and there the child Independence was born."[38]

A Great Fire Snuffed Out

Four years after his impassioned oratory failed to win over the King's judges, James Otis had not abandoned the cause of freedom. And more and more Bostonians seemed to be coming to his side. Dissatisfaction with the colonial rulers was growing, but those loyal to the Crown remained firmly entrenched. Each side had its preferred gathering places around town, and when members of one faction found themselves on the other's turf, there was bound to be trouble.

The solidly loyalist British Coffee House lay barely a block from the seat of government in colonial Massachusetts—the brick, two-story Old Town House. On this Friday evening of September 5, 1765, some gentlemen may have leisurely sauntered into its friendly confines, puffing on their clay pipes, dipping their snuff, and contentedly counting on an autumn evening of nothing more than bracing coffee and pleasant conversation.

But not James Otis Jr.

He was mad.

At just past seven, James Otis strode into the coffeehouse. This establishment was hardly his usual haunt. He, along with such other patriots as Paul Revere, John Adams, and John Hancock, normally gathered at the two-storied, brick Green Dragon on Union Street in Boston's North End, an establishment Daniel Webster would later dub "the headquarters of the Revolution."[39] High loyalist officials and their British officer friends, on the other hand, favored the British Coffee House. For James Otis to enter their den—particularly on this night—required high courage.

Otis's patriotic fire had only grown since his famous case against the writs of assistance. Boston's royal officials were still running rough-shod over the rights of their fellow Englishmen just because they happened to be American colonists—and Otis had never stopped fighting back. A friend to the Boston patriots, he wrote a number of pamphlets extolling the virtues of liberty. In 1764 he even wrote that America's "colonists are by the law of nature free born, as indeed all men are, white or black. . . . Does it follow that tis right to enslave a man because he is black?"[40] Now he was facing the consequences for his expansive view of liberty—and upping the ante.

Upset by his activism, important people in the government, particularly high-ranking officials in the royal customs service, had started a behind-the-scenes campaign against him—bad-mouthing him, working to undermine his reputation, even to the point of essentially accusing him of treason.

Otis decided not to let the charges stand and responded publicly. The night before this visit to the British Coffee House, he had placed an advertisement in the patriot-friendly *Boston Gazette* (its logo designed by Paul Revere; its motto: "Containing the freshest Advices, Foreign and Domestic"). The notice did not mince words.

Otis listed four royal customs officers by name—"Henry Hutton, Charles Paxton, William Burch, and John Robinson, Esquires"—and announced that they had "treated the characters of all true North Americans in a manner that is not to be endured, by privately and publicly representing them as traitors and rebels, and in a general combination to revolt from Great Britain." Not only that, Otis stated, these four had targeted him personally as well. "Without the least provocation or colour," he said, they "have represented me by name, as inimical to the rights of the crown, and disaffected to his majesty, to whom I annually swear, and am determined at all events to bear true, and faithful allegiance." Otis's frustration is understandable. At this point, though he and other patriots were agitating for their rights as Englishmen, they still viewed themselves as just that—Englishmen.

In the face of this "general, as well as personal abuse and insult," Otis informed the *Gazette* readers, "Satisfaction has been personally demanded, due warning given, but no sufficient answer obtained." Though he had not received his own satisfaction, Otis could still issue a call to anyone "who may condescend to read this, to pay no kind of regard to any of the abusive representations of me or my country, that may be transmitted" by the four miscreant officials "or their confederates." He added that "they are no more worthy of credit, than those of Sir Francis Bernard . . . or any of his cabal"—taking a swipe at Massachusetts' sitting royal governor for good measure. And this was no anonymous screed—the name at the bottom read simply: "James Otis."[41]

There it was—in print. Otis's public naming and shaming of the King's customs officers who sought to slander him with "personal abuse and insult," as well as his notice that "satisfaction has been personally demanded," was circulating around Boston, the word spreading to readers all over the city that James Otis was not going to take these "abusive representations" lying down. Notably, Otis was not just out to avenge his own personal honor as a gentleman. Otis took issue with the customs agents' attitude toward his fellow colonists, making sure to stand up for "all true North Americans" against remarks made against not just himself, but "my country" as well.

On this visit to the British Coffee House, Otis would come face-to-face with one of his slanderers.

Sitting inside was John Robinson, one of the quartet of royal officials Otis had dared to excoriate in his *Boston Gazette* advertisement the day before. Whether Robinson anticipated Otis's arrival we will never know, but we do know this: almost instantly the two launched into a duel of harsh, biting words. When Robinson looked up and saw Otis, he immediately let loose a torrent of abuse.[42]

One account published in a British newspaper at the time said that Otis suggested they discuss the matter in a private room. Robinson agreed, "very unexpectedly to Mr. Otis."[43] But as Otis got up from his seat, Robinson lashed out, grabbing at Otis's nose.[44] When he missed, he raised his cane and struck Otis with it. Quickly, Robinson's friends in the coffeehouse sprang from their seats—their chairs crashing behind them—and charged into the fray. Otis was set upon and beaten mercilessly with walking canes and fists, with cudgels, and most likely even slashed with a sword. "The general cry," according to the *London Chronicle*, was "*Kill him! Kill him!*"

Another patron named John Gridley, seeing Otis set upon by such unfair numbers, rushed in to assist him. It was no use. The crowd turned on young Gridley, tendering him blow after blow, and tossing him back outside.

Eventually, the struggle became so intense that not only could Otis not defend himself, but he could not even flee his attackers. The *Massachusetts Gazette* reported that he "received many very heavy blows on his head, and one particularly on his forehead, that instantly produced a copious discharge of blood."[45] He was too injured to manage any escape and was at the mercy of the royalist mob until its members decided that they'd had enough and slunk out the back door. His friends found him lying senseless on the floor of the British Coffee House and carried his nearly lifeless body back toward his home. If he had not been carried away immediately, the *Massachusetts Gazette* indicated, "the consequence of this ungenerous assault would have been fatal."[46] Worst of all his many injuries was a massive head wound, a gash so large that "you could lay a finger in it."[47]

Long before his fellow patriots pledged their lives, fortunes, and sacred honor to the cause of independence, James Otis Jr. had paid a very large price for his love for liberty and the rights of man, and for daring to stand up for himself and his fellow American colonists in the pages of the *Boston Gazette*.

When these royal officials struck back violently against James Otis for standing up to them, they began the slow, tortuous process of erasing him from history. The violence that had been visited on Otis was to leave its mark on him for the remainder of his life. Though he lived on for nearly two more decades after this altercation, his mental health went into decline over the next few years, and his role in the colony's public life had dwindled by 1769. The massive blow to his head is thought to be at least partially responsible for this. "The wound he had received," according to an early biographer, "rendered him extremely susceptible to excitement, and deep thinking would easily inflame him"—a real tragedy for a mind as brilliant as Otis's.[48] By January 1770, John Adams would note that Otis, when speaking, "rambles and wanders like a Ship without an Helm. . . . I fear he is not in his perfect Mind."[49]

He still came in and out of lucid periods, but the eccentricities were troubling. In one episode, he destroyed nearly all of his personal papers and letters over the course of two days, robbing history of a great resource and, in effect, helping to blot out his own legacy.[50]

This tortured genius of the early revolution did manage to die in a dramatic fashion: he was struck by lightning while standing in his doorway in 1783, before he could see the republic finally take shape. Interestingly enough, he is said to have told his sister, Mercy Otis Warren, just weeks before his death: "My dear sister, I hope, when God Almighty in his righteous providence shall take me out of time into eternity that it will be by a flash of lightning."[51] Otis himself flashed into the Revolution like a bolt of lightning—one that sadly disappeared too quickly. Nevertheless, his efforts against unlawful searches and seizures—later enshrined in the Constitution—created powerful aftershocks that echoed down the centuries.

If the "child Independence" was born from Otis's case against the writs of assistance, it is sobering to consider that, centuries later, we are still grappling with the same issue. Where Otis was concerned about customs officials abusing writs to break into someone's premises and rifle through his papers, today raises similar concerns about the safety of the digital "papers" we keep on our computers or in online cloud storage. In a time of dangerous national security challenges, government surveillance against American citizens remains a threat. Holding government accountable for using these capabilities responsibly and within constitutional boundaries remains an important task.

It is enjoyable to imagine Otis himself arguing before a secret Foreign Intelligence Surveillance Act court. While we don't have James Otis, we have the Fourth Amendment, designed to combat the same abuses Otis fought against, to guide us. But we almost didn't even get that. The Fourth Amendment, along with the rest of the Bill of Rights, was enacted only after the strenuous efforts of some individuals who believed that the Constitution, as initially adopted, did not go far enough to protect our rights.

CHAPTER 8

George Mason: Defender of Individual and Economic Freedom

THE KING HAD SHUT DOWN THE LAWFUL LEGISLATIVE BODY OF his Virginian colonists, but that wasn't going to stop the representatives themselves from meeting. Instead of the more dignified confines of their official chambers, they now found themselves in more rough-hewn (but cozier) surroundings. The smells that enveloped them were no longer those of ink and fresh parchment and musty old law books, but instead those of ale and baking bread.

On May 17, 1769, the Virginia House of Burgesses had convened in Williamsburg and passed resolutions declaring that British Parliament had no right to levy taxes on the colonists or otherwise interfere with colonial commerce. Following instructions from the Crown, the governor responded by dissolving the House of Burgesses. The members, now the "late representatives of the people," adjourned to the Raleigh Tavern in Williamsburg, where they "adopted an 'Association,' based in part on a draft by one of the most scholarly among their friends, a northern Virginia planter named George Mason. Mason's neighbor, George Washington, had carried that document to the meeting in his pocket."[1] Also known as the "Non-Importation Agreement," the plan called for a boycott of all British goods that included taxes. There were those, including Mason himself, who pressed even further for a ban on the shipment of colonially produced goods—such as the very tobacco he grew—to England.

As a fourth-generation colonist, George Mason IV was plenty proud of his British roots. Despite headaches caused by sporadic meddling from the Crown, life in the New World had proved prosperous for him and his family. At the age of forty-three, he also enjoyed the same political prestige (in Virginia and beyond) that the three George Masons before him had. In addition, Mason was revered as something of an elder statesman because of his age. He was seven years older than his close neighbor George Washington, who had become a confidant and business associate. In 1752 Mason had begun building his small but stately Gunston Hall, overlooking the Potomac River just a few miles down from Washington's Mount Vernon. Mason was eighteen years older than another influential Virginian, Thomas Jefferson. Jefferson looked up to Mason as well, and would later openly credit the older gentleman as the inspiration for the immortal words that would open the Declaration of Independence. And Mason was a full twenty-five years older than James Madison, who would finally prevail in the fight initially led by Mason to adopt a bill of rights, designed to further curtail the powers of the federal government.

By 1769 Mason—though still a proud British subject and still loyal to the King—found himself increasingly concerned with what he considered warrantless meddling from across the sea. And while the wildfire of the American Revolution would at times burn hottest over personal liberty, religious freedom, and local self-government, the earliest sparks were over taxation and freedom of commerce. Increasingly, the British government levied more taxes on the colonists and tried to establish regulation and inspection schemes as a means of collecting those taxes.

This illicit gathering inside Raleigh Tavern—a busy and convivial pub that would become a famous gathering place for revolutionaries—was significant not only because of *what* transpired there (the Non-

Importation Agreement), but also because of *who* had participated in such open defiance of the Crown. For decades, the colonies had endured recessions, and people from every walk of life had blamed the recessions on perpetual interference from Parliament and the King. Constant efforts to regulate and tax tobacco or sugar or tea were met with deep resentment from the colonists. Though the 1773 Boston Tea Party was the most famous, there were many other instances of angry colonial mobs burning wharves and protesting taxes, regulations, and other economic interferences from London. What was different about this meeting in Williamsburg in 1769 was that this was no angry mob of struggling tenant farmers. These men gathered at the Raleigh Tavern were some of the most prosperous, influential people of the day. Thomas Jefferson, Patrick Henry, and Edmund Randolph were among them. And all of them had had enough.

Although Mason was not even a member of the House of Burgesses at the time—he had quit after just one term almost a decade earlier—his presence at the Raleigh Tavern meeting carried enormous weight with those still serving, including Washington himself. Throughout his life, Mason held a complicated view of public service. As would later become apparent to all who knew him, he was deeply passionate about the shape a government should take. While he believed government should promote the free exchange of commerce, he vigorously maintained that the powers of government must be subject to strict limitations. Mason insisted that, in the absence of faithfully observed and aggressively enforced constraints, governments invariably overreach, harming the people by (among other things) undermining personal and religious freedom.

Given his generally dim view of government, Mason considered actually serving in any public capacity not only tiresome but also a waste of time. He had very little patience for committee meetings and all the "babblers."[2]

In 1790, near the end of his life, Mason refused an appointment to serve in the newly formed United States Senate, preferring to remain at home with his chores and his family. Just like his father before him, Mason directed most of his passion toward his family, his sprawling plantation, and his wide array of business interests that reached all the way to the frontier with the Ohio Company. A royal grant of some two hundred thousand acres along the Ohio River (around what is today Pittsburgh, Pennsylvania), the Ohio Company occupied much of Mason's time and attention for more than forty years, highlighting his profound belief in the power of free commerce to develop a new country.

Despite his unconcealed contempt for public life and even public service, Mason would be constantly drawn into public matters. This was partly due to his uncommon political intelligence, but it was also owing to his deep and abiding interest in all manner of free commerce.

In 1785 officials in Maryland and Virginia convened a conference to establish a set of rules governing the Potomac River that flowed between the two states.[3] The first conference was held at George Washington's Mount Vernon in March of that year. Washington himself personally suggested that George Mason attend. In less than a week, Mason, Washington, and the other delegates would agree on a thirteen-point plan to solve the thorniest navigational issues between the two colonies. Both states' legislatures would approve of the pact before year's end. The so-called Mount Vernon Compact would become proof that two colonies could manage their interstate commerce perfectly well without the meddling from an intrusive, distant central government. But the success of the conference at Mount Vernon also became the hopeful model for a grander, broader convention—one that would lay the groundwork for a much larger, stronger federal government capable of regulating trade between all thirteen colonies.

But for the men in the Raleigh Tavern in 1769, this would have been nearly impossible to fathom. Any such grand plans for the future could not have been further from George Mason's mind as he gathered with George Washington and the other former Burgesses to repeal the myriad taxes and regulations placed upon the colonies by the British Parliament and the Crown. It is worth noting that at the time, though they hoped for relief from unfair taxes, those gathered at the tavern still remained loyal subjects, toasting the health of the King and his family, along with that of the governor, and expressing their wish for "a speedy and lasting Union between Great-Britain and her Colonies."[4]

For a while, it looked as if harmony would be restored. In fairly short order, after the Non-Importation Agreement was approved, the British blinked. They repealed almost all the taxes and regulations placed upon the colonies—*almost* all of them: except for the tax on tea.

"All Men Are by Nature Equally Free and Independent"

As George Mason's carriage jostled along the bumpy road south to Williamsburg, a teeming medley of thoughts simultaneously bounced around his mind. As was his nature, he was working diligently to bring them into order. He knew that he would have to hit the ground running as soon as he made it to the Virginia Assembly then in session—there was no time to waste. As the horses surged forward, Mason's excitement surged on with them.

There had been moments recently when he had regretted not

joining young Thomas Jefferson and the others in the Virginia delegation to the Continental Congress in Philadelphia. By this time, in
May 1776, Mason's world was in the grip of heady change, and some
part of him wanted a hand in the effort—despite his hatred for the
political game.

The seething fervor for revolution in the colonies had turned into
a full-blown conflagration. Even families of great wealth and influence like the Masons, who had been subjects of the King and
Parliament for generations and were proud of their British heritage,
had had enough of the indignities of living at the whim of a king and
an increasingly tax-hungry Parliament in a faraway land. In New
England, the tensions had finally spilled over into a shooting war the
year before when the musket balls flew at Lexington and Concord.

The same year that open hostilities broke out, in 1775, George
Mason had been pressed to accept an appointment to the Continental Congress to represent Virginia. He refused. While the American
colonies experienced earth-shattering change by going to war with
Great Britain, Mason's own world had been shattered two years
previously. In 1773 Ann Eilbeck Mason, his devoted wife and the
mother of his children, had died from complications after childbirth.
He was now a single father of nine children. In addition, he still had
his full-time occupation running his sprawling Gunston Hall plantation on the Potomac River. For Mason, a trip to Philadelphia was
out of the cards. Home and family simply had to come first.

But on May 15, 1776, Virginia directed its delegates in the Continental Congress to propose independence. But if the Virginians
were going to make such a bold move, they could not leave their
fellow colonists without some sort of guide as to what an independent
future might look like. It was decided that the Virginia delegations
would be tasked with drawing up a Declaration of Rights, along with
the early framings of a government. But whatever the representatives

in Philadelphia came up with would have to be approved by the delegates to state conventions.

This was a call George Mason could not ignore.

Recovering from another of his endless physical ailments—usually a bout of gout combined with one or more other maladies—Mason set out for Williamsburg, where state conventioneers geared up for revolution.

He arrived in the city and was promptly placed on the committee to draft a Declaration of Rights for Virginia.

Mason came prepared. His thoughts had ordered themselves, and he immediately took charge of the proceedings. Plenty of progress had been made on the Declaration of Rights by those already on hand, such as Patrick Henry, Edmund Randolph, James Madison, and two dozen other illustrious Virginians. In short order, the work of George Mason "swallowed up all the rest," Randolph would later report.

Edmund Pendleton, president of the Virginia Assembly in Williamsburg, eagerly conveyed the good news to Thomas Jefferson, who was toiling away on a similar such document in Philadelphia.

"[T]he political cooks are busy in preparing the dish, and as Colonel Mason seems to have the ascendancy in the great work, I have sanguine hopes it will be framed so as to answer its end," he wrote Jefferson.[5]

Mason's Virginia Declaration of Rights drew upon the timeless wisdom found in the Magna Carta and other bills of rights, as well as all the writings of political philosophers, both ancient and modern. What made it stand out as an altogether new and more dangerous clarion call for freedom was its unabashed emphasis on the personal rights of every individual. Its bold language and sweeping, subversive contentions would pose an immediate threat to any king. But it was even more ahead of its time in another way. By Mason's careful calculation, the document contained language that would eventually pose a threat to any man wishing to own another.

"Mason's strictures on equality, the citizen's inalienable right to life and liberty—he added the pursuit of happiness—and his idea that magistrates were trustees of the people's rights came directly from John Locke," biographer Jeff Broadwater would later write. "Part of the genius of the Declaration of Rights lay in Mason's ability to combine Enlightenment political philosophy with the English legal tradition to express in scarcely two pages the ideology of the American Revolution."[6] With his Declaration of Rights, Mason proved himself "a transitional figure in a period during which liberal thought was shifting from an emphasis on representative government to a concern for individual rights."[7]

Within weeks—on June 12, 1776—Mason's declaration was unanimously adopted by the Virginia convention. Mason then got to work on the state's constitution.

Meanwhile, three hundred miles north over hellish carriage roads, Thomas Jefferson and the other delegates to the Continental Convention eagerly devoured Mason's work, dispatched with all haste from Williamsburg. They immediately began incorporating the elder statesman's language into their own Declaration of Independence, which would soon utterly dwarf the fame and prestige of their state's Declaration of Rights.

Jefferson famously wrote, "We hold these truths to be self-evident, that all men are created equal, that they are endowed by their Creator with certain unalienable rights, that among these are Life, Liberty and the pursuit of Happiness."

It was a clear nod to Mason's own declaration that "all men are by nature equally free and independent, and have certain inherent rights of which . . . they cannot deprive or divest their posterity;

namely, the enjoyment of life and liberty, with the means of acquiring and possessing property, and pursuing and obtaining happiness and safety."

Jefferson's Declaration of Independence would not be the last time George Mason's declaration would be copied. Echoes can be found in the U.S. Bill of Rights—the amendments passed between 1789 and 1791, thanks in part to Mason's strong support—as well as the Declaration of the Rights of Man and the Citizen issued during the French Revolution and even the Universal Declaration of Human Rights passed by the United Nations more than 150 years later.

Students today may be forgiven for thinking this all sounds nice and quaint, after nearly 250 years of unprecedented religious and personal freedom. But in their day, these were, indeed, radical concepts that would soon overturn millennia of political thinking and centuries of political structures. The despotic monarchies that were the norm around the world could now be challenged. But proposing such dangerous political blasphemy would surely not come without threat to life, family, and treasure.

Five years after penning the Virginia Declaration of Rights, Mason would find himself beset, at home in Gunston Hall along the Potomac River, by British warships stalking up and down the waterway "within two or three miles of Alexandria," meaning offshore from Gunston Hall as well as from George Washington's Mount Vernon.

"The Enemy is now professedly carrying on a predatory war against Us," he warned in a letter to Virginia delegates in Philadelphia. "Private people have lately been robbed, their Houses burned, & their Estates ruined by the Crews of British Ships." And, most ominously, he warned that the enemy was now "preparing a great number of flat-bottomed Boats at Portsmouth, notoriously for the purpose of plundering the Tobacco warehouses & the Inhabitants upon the Rivers & Creeks in Virginia & Maryland."[8]

It was war—even for civilians—and everything George Mason cherished in this world was at stake.

"I Would Sooner Chop Off My Right Hand Than Put It to the Constitution as It Now Stands"

Another political crisis, another jostling carriage journey: this time George Mason was traveling north, not south—to Philadelphia, not Williamsburg. Finally, the sage of the Potomac had been persuaded to dislodge himself from his peaceful, prosperous home life and travel hundreds of miles to throw himself fully into the fires forging his new nation. And fire may well have been on his mind— that spring and summer in Philadelphia was exceptionally hot. It would have been characteristic of Mason, stuffed in his airless carriage, to make a note to himself to remark upon this discomfort to his fellow delegates when he arrived.

It was not as though Mason had avoided the revolutionary ferment that had lately gripped Virginia and the other onetime colonies, now states. He had not been able to completely resist the entreaties from neighbors and fellow countrymen to join in the airing of grievances against the King and Parliament. Then came the rabble-rousing and saber rattling, and Mason found himself in the middle of it. When it came time, at last, to demand independence, Mason was there leading the charge. In war, Mason put his considerable organizational skills to use in helping keep the Continental Army fed, clothed, and armed. And when it came time to form a new government, Mason yet again found himself pressed into service. After every new venture, Mason hurried home to Gunston Hall, sometimes even before business was finished. For as much of an elder statesman and gentleman revolutionary as he may have been, he himself was mostly consumed with what he felt was his highest calling: to be a private family man, with sprawling business interests along both sides of the vast and unforgiving Potomac River.

But this time something was different. In spite of his occasional contrary nature, Mason found himself—even if he was loath to admit it—looking forward to his trip to Pennsylvania.

No matter how much George Mason hated the tedium of political wrangling, and despised being taken away from his family and his many commercial demands at Gunston Hall—which was now the seat of some twenty-four thousand acres of farming—he kept getting pulled back into the arena he had tried so hard to avoid.

With the Virginia Declaration of Rights and the state's constitution completed, and with navigational agreements between Virginia and Maryland in place, Mason was ready to retire from public life for good. But pressure was mounting. Delegates were planning to gather once again in Philadelphia to amend the Articles of Confederation. George Mason was, as before, under tremendous pressure to join the effort.

Mason had always found the endless debates of such conventions tedious, and the most long-winded orators downright aggravating. When fellow Virginians succeeded in coercing him into going—often that unpleasant duty fell to Mason's neighbor George Washington—Mason would show up late and leave early. Drafting the Virginia Declaration of Rights had been just his kind of work—delivering in a quick burst of genius a top-quality document churned out with great efficiency, a mission swiftly accomplished. When his work kept him away for long periods, his family had come to expect his complaining about the tedium for days and weeks after his return.

After one such state convention in Virginia, he saw fit to remind George Washington of just how awful the experience had been for him, complaining that "Mere Vexation & Disgust threw me into such an ill state of health that before the Convention rose, I was sometimes near fainting in the House."[9]

But as the Continental Convention in Philadelphia drew near, Mason showed "unexpected stamina and surprising vigor."[10] On May 17, 1787, George Mason arrived at the convention, ready to work.

Though Mason would eventually come to fiercely oppose the proposed Constitution and refuse to sign it, he worked diligently through the entire long, hot summer. And despite his uncharacteristic optimism toward the task at hand, Mason found plenty to complain about.

"He had never been so far away from home, never been in a large city, and never seen a real merchant aristocracy," historian Jeff Broadwater wrote later. "He soon grew 'heartily tired of the etiquette and nonsense so fashionable in this city.'"[11]

But inside the Pennsylvania State House, Mason proved agreeable and eager to compromise. For weeks and then months, delegates hammered out the basic outlines of a new national government. The broad strokes of a two-chambered legislature, a judiciary, and an executive branch were roughly framed. Mason certainly found issue and disagreement with plenty of the points, but by July 26, when the convention adjourned to prepare a report on progress, Mason appeared still to be on board. And by all accounts, he had contributed enormously to the yet-unfinished draft.

Once the convention resumed, George Mason got back to making his helpful and hopeful contributions. Up to that moment, so much of the debate had been about parliamentary facets of the emerging government. But as August wore on, Mason found himself repeatedly on the losing end of the most important issues nearest to his heart: free and open commerce.

Mason could debate the finer points of whether the executive branch should be headed by one person or three—and he did!—but what really mattered to the Virginia planter was an assurance that this burgeoning new monstrosity would leave people's business interests alone.

For instance, he wanted the new constitution to specifically prohibit Congress from imposing any sort of taxes on exports. Even a compromise requiring taxes to be approved by a two-thirds supermajority vote in both houses of Congress failed. It failed narrowly, but it failed nonetheless.

One compromise whose failure was especially troubling to Mason involved congressional meddling in navigation acts, which Mason viewed as a backdoor attempt at taxing exports. Mason, after all, was an expert on interstate commerce, being a merchant himself and having painstakingly negotiated trade deals between Virginia and Maryland.

Empowering Congress to enact laws "by a bare majority," Mason argued on September 15, "would enable a few rich merchants in Philadelphia, New York and Boston, to monopolize the staples of the Southern States, and reduce their value perhaps fifty percent."[12]

He urged fellow delegates in Philadelphia to prohibit any such "navigation acts" before the year 1808 without the consent of two-thirds support in both the House and the Senate. In other words, Mason wanted to set a very high bar for allowing the federal government to interfere with commerce between the states and abroad.

Unfortunately for Mason, his was a lonely voice. Only his native Virginia, along with Maryland (whose delegates were certainly aware of Mason's interstate commerce expertise) and Georgia shared his fear of federal interference in trade, and voted in favor of his motion.

The rest of the Southern states that should have shared Mason's fear of unfettered federal control over commerce had, it turned out, made a dirty side deal with industrial Northern states—one that would keep the booming slave trade in business. Mason would later recall with considerable regret how he lost the fight.

"This business was discussed at Philadelphia for four months, during which time the subject of commerce and navigation was often under consideration," he recalled to delegates to the Virginia ratifying convention. "Eight states out of twelve, for more than three months, voted for requiring two-thirds of the members present in each House to pass commercial and navigation laws. If I am right, there was a great majority for requiring two-thirds of the States in this business, till a compromise took place between the Northern and Southern States; the Northern States agreeing to the temporary importation of slaves, and the Southern States conceding, in return, that navigation and commercial laws should be on the footing on which they now stand."[13]

These debates over the government's role in navigation and trade would eventually result in the Constitution's Commerce Clause—in Article I, Section 8—which gives Congress the power "to regulate Commerce with foreign Nations, and among the several States, and with the Indian Tribes."

Mason's frustrations came to a blistering head when the debate turned to slavery. Mason, himself an owner of slaves, called for an immediate end to the importation of new slaves.

"Every master of slaves is born a petty tyrant," Mason declared. "They bring the judgement of Heaven on a country. As nations cannot be rewarded or punished in the next world, they must be in this. By an inevitable chain of causes and effects, Providence punishes national sins by national calamities."[14]

Needless to say, this excoriation of slavery was met with hostile opposition from his fellow Southerners. And Mason's fellow delegates from the North were all too happy to keep the slave trade alive if it meant they could get something of their own in the bargain.

And what the Yankees wanted was to allow Congress a free hand in passing navigation regulations.[15]

"Throughout most of August, Mason maintained his position of positive participation," historian Helen Hill Miller writes. "Only after the deal on commercial regulations and the slave trade did his speeches, along with those of various other delegates, begin to show a growing restiveness."[16]

At this point, Mason and his fellow Anti-Federalists began meeting separately in private to discuss their growing grievances.

The final straw for Mason came September 12 when "the Convention as a whole and his own delegation in particular dealt him a major humiliation."[17]

Mason proposed that any constitution be preceded by a very specific bill of rights.

"It would give great quiet to the people," he argued. "And with the aid of the state declarations, a bill might be prepared in a few hours."[18]

Elbridge Gerry gamely spoke up in support and moved for the creation of a committee to draft such a bill. Mason seconded, but the proposal was unanimously rejected—every state voted no, except Massachusetts, which abstained.

Though Mason continued to work toward completing the document, he had now turned bitterly against the proposed Constitution. He feared that the behemoth new government would trample the most basic individual liberties and would become every bit as tax-hungry as the previous tyrant. And he was certain that the Leviathan would eventually encumber free commerce in an endless web of taxes and regulation, strangling the great engine of American innovation.

On August 31, two weeks before the delegates would finish their work in Philadelphia, Mason rose to address the convention.

He would, he told them, "sooner chop off his right hand than put it to the Constitution as it now stands. There is no declaration of rights. There is no declaration of any kind for preserving the liberty of the press, the trial by jury in civil cases, nor the danger of standing armies in time of peace."[19]

By the time the convention wrapped up, Mason was wholly lost. He left Philadelphia, according to James Madison, "in an exceedingly ill humor."[20] On the long, rough journey home, as he and a fellow delegate from Maryland approached Baltimore, Mason's carriage overturned, injuring Mason seriously enough for him to require medical attention. It was one final insult to end a long summer of disappointment.

Mason would go on from the convention to campaign heartily against ratification of the new Constitution. When he detailed his arguments in a pamphlet entitled *Objections to This Constitution of Government*—the original draft of which he composed while still in Philadelphia, on the back of a draft copy of the Constitution— the lack of a bill of rights was listed first and foremost:

"There is no Declaration of Rights, and the laws of the general government being paramount to the laws and constitution of the several States, the Declarations of Rights in the separate States are no security. Nor are the people secured even in the enjoyment of the benefit of the common law." He added later: "There is no declaration of any kind, for preserving the liberty of the press, or the trial by jury in civil causes; nor against the danger of standing armies in time of peace."[21]

Among his arguments, too, were the flaws of the "navigation act" structure:

> By requiring only a majority to make all commercial and navigation laws, the five Southern States, whose produce and circumstances are totally different from that of the eight Northern and Eastern States, may be ruined, for such rigid and premature regulations may be made as will enable the merchants of the Northern and Eastern States not only to demand an exhorbitant freight, but to monopolize the purchase of the commodities at their own price, for many years, to the great injury of the landed interest, and impoverishment of the people; and the danger is the greater as the gain on one side will be in proportion to the loss on the other. Whereas requiring two-thirds of the members present in both Houses would have produced mutual moderation, promoted the general interest, and removed an insuperable objection to the adoption of this government.[22]

And then, using his own brilliant rhetorical flair, he brought it all together in a synthesis of the arguments for greater individual and economic freedom:

"Under their own construction of the general clause, at the end of the enumerated powers, the Congress may grant monopolies in trade and commerce, constitute new crimes, inflict unusual and severe punishments, and extend their powers as far as they shall think proper; so that the State legislatures have no security for the powers now presumed to remain to them, or the people for their rights."[23]

Ultimately, Mason would lose the fight against ratification, too, the following year in his home state of Virginia. His only consolation was that his much younger fellow Virginian James Madison seemed determined to make good on promises to eventually adopt the Bill of Rights to the Constitution, which he succeeded in doing in 1791.

A Nation Forged, a Friendship Shattered

The air was cool and pleasant that early morning in the spring of 1792, and George Mason paused to enjoy it as he stepped out onto the small back porch of his beloved Gunston Hall. He had just come from his private library, his favorite room in the house that had been his home for the last four decades. From the porch he could see the elaborate English boxwood gardens that he and his first wife, the wise, gentle, and beautiful Ann, had planted together before her untimely death some nineteen years earlier. Though Mason eventually remarried, he never got over his first true love.

"She was blessed with a clear and sound judgment, a gentle and benevolent heart, a sincere and a humble mind, with an even, calm and cheerful temper to a very unusual degree; affable to all, but intimate with few," Mason wrote in the family Bible after she died.[24]

"Her modest virtue shunned the public eye; superior to the turbulent passions of pride and envy, a stranger to altercation of any kind, and content with the blessings of a private station, she placed all her happiness here, where only it is to be found, in her own family. Though she despised dress, she was always neat; cheerful, but not gay; serious, but not melancholy; she never met me without a smile! Though an only child, she was a remarkably dutiful one. An easy and agreeable companion, a kind neighbor, a steadfast friend, a humane mistress, a prudent and tender mother, a faithful, affectionate, and most obliging wife; charitable to the poor, and pious to her Maker; her virtue and religion were unmixed with hypocrisy or ostentation."[25]

It was a heartfelt eulogy, yet now Mason wondered, as he sometimes did, whether his mere words were able to do her justice. At least a part of her lived on in their nine surviving children, all of whom were now grown.

Off to his right he could see the small, modest grave where Ann had been laid to rest. The boxwoods before him were a pastel green from the new spring growth. Beyond the garden, the lawn tumbled steeply to the southeast, before leveling out a little at the vast deer park below the house. In the far distance, Mason could view the sun glinting off the Potomac River, swollen with the heavy spring rains.

To his left—some five miles upriver and out of sight—lived his neighbor, George Washington. The two had known each other for more than a generation, and their friendship had been sometimes warm but often complicated. By this point, however, after so many disagreements stemming from the Constitutional Convention and ratification, it had grown flat-out cold. Mason, a somewhat portly fellow who was prone to severe bouts of gout and other illnesses common in that era, had always been revered by Washington and many of their colleagues in the early American Republic for his deep and broad knowledge of politics and government. Thomas Jefferson credited him with the inspiration for the Declaration of Independence. Everyone credited him for his considerable contributions to the federal Constitution.

But as Washington and others had learned firsthand, Mason's knowledge and wisdom came at a price. He was highly principled but also hugely stubborn. He could be maddeningly intractable, an immovable object immune to appeals for compromise. In Philadelphia in 1787, when it had come time to rally behind all their hard work and sign the new federal Constitution, Mason refused. Not only did he decline to put his name to the document he was so instrumental in crafting, but he harangued aggressively against it. And then went home and vigorously lobbied his fellow Virginians to refuse to ratify the document that would organize a new federal government.

His reasoning had been sound and his conscience clear. He had hoped to use the new Constitution to bring an immediate end to the slave trade, and it had not. Though Mason himself owned dozens of slaves, he was acutely aware that slavery was incompatible with the radical principles upon which this new country was to be founded. More deeply, he viewed slavery as a poison that rotted the souls of slaveholders—a poison of which he wanted to purge both his country and himself.

His principled concerns led him to take other difficult stances as well, with equal seriousness. He had flatly refused to sign or support any proposed constitution that did not spell out a specific list of rights and protections for individual freedom and religious liberties. He was deeply concerned that the powerful and unchecked federal government would invariably seek to accumulate power at the ultimate and endless expense of the states, and therefore the people. This would go on to hamper economic growth in the states, which Mason knew would be the engine that drove the fledgling nation. Mason viewed a powerful federal government as the greatest enemy to a vital economy.

As he glanced upriver in the direction of Washington's home at Mount Vernon, Mason breathed a quiet sigh of dismay over the breakdown of relations with his fellow Virginian. As a man now very conscious of his own advanced years, he abhorred the thought of leaving rancor behind him when he left the mortal plane. He tried to suppress painful thoughts of his disagreement with Washington at Philadelphia, wondering all the while whether there was any hope of reconciliation. He had visited Washington at Mount Vernon in 1788, but just a year later wrote to his son John Mason of "the friendship which has long existed (indeed from our early youth) between General Washington and myself," lamenting that "it is possible my opposition to the new government, both as a member of the national and of the Virginia Convention, may have altered the case."[26]

Regrettably, when Mason died in that fall of 1792 inside his beloved home high on the Potomac bluffs, he and Washington were still estranged.

That was the price Mason paid for his principles, for his unyielding—or what some may call "stubborn"—commitment to the things that matter. It is perfectly logical for any good American to be "stubborn" about things like individual liberties, as George Mason was—stubborn enough to refuse to sign the nation's governing document (which Mason himself had helped draft!), stubborn enough to break ties with a longtime friend and neighbor. Mason's example reminds us that sometimes one has to be stubborn in defense of one's principles.

Today far too many of us, especially in Washington, seem to have lost sight of that. That stands as evidence of George Mason's legacy having shamefully faded from history. George Washington's Mount Vernon, just a few short miles up the Potomac, is one of the most frequently visited historic sites in the nation—yet George Mason's lovingly preserved Gunston Hall is often overlooked by the tourists who flock to the area.

A prominent international travel guide's entry on Gunston Hall concedes that Mason is "not well known outside Virginia."[27] A travel writer in a major newspaper opened a 2016 piece on Gunston Hall by declaring that "Mount Vernon tends to get all the attention when it comes to historic homes in the Washington, DC, area, and deservedly so," before describing Mason's home as "not nearly as fancy, or large, as that of his Fairfax County neighbor's."[28]

Could Mason have been diminished because he was on the wrong side of a dispute with such an august figure as George Washington? Did his contrarian stance on individual liberties during the debate over the Constitution—which was ultimately vindicated in the Bill of Rights—contribute to his being dismissed as "not well known outside Virginia"? Considering how strongly Mason felt about his principles, and how much he enjoyed being left alone in his native state, perhaps being "written out" would not have bothered him after all.

CONCLUSION

Writing Our Forgotten Founders Back into History

GOVERNMENTS ARE ALL ABOUT FORCE. IT THEREFORE SHOULD NOT be surprising that throughout human history, governments have caused immeasurable suffering. That, of course, does not mean that government is inherently evil. It simply means that—like fire— government must be approached not only with a full understanding of its usefulness, but also with a healthy respect for the dangers it presents. Unlike fire, however, government is more than a force that is routinely *harnessed by* human beings; government *consists of* human beings. No government can exist or act independently of people; its actions are those of the human beings who administer and support it. For that very reason, despite the lofty, aspirational rhetoric routinely employed by governments—rhetoric designed to encourage an almost religious faith in government itself—we cannot fully understand government without remembering that governments are neither autonomous nor omniscient nor omnipotent; they are operated entirely by mere mortals. Thus, we cannot navigate the risks presented by government without taking into account human nature.

Human beings are flawed. They make mistakes. Many of the decisions they make are based on incomplete information. They engage in self-interested behavior, especially as they compete for scarce resources. They have a tendency to mistreat one another, sometimes maliciously. They tend to covet the power and possessions of others.

Despite these flaws, human beings are redeemable. Each person has a soul and will one day stand accountable to God for his own actions on earth. But even in this life, individuals can learn to pursue their own interests while simultaneously advancing (or at least without harming) the interests of others. When people are allowed to interact freely in pursuit of their own well-being, they tend to prosper—that is, as long as they understand that they may not violate the life, liberty, and property of others, and that they will face unpleasant consequences if they try to do so.

That's where government comes into play. Through government, people can establish and enforce rules to protect the natural rights (that is, life, liberty, and property) of each individual. A government that succeeds in protecting natural rights promotes the prosperity of its people by encouraging citizens to engage in productive, self-interested behavior in a way that does not harm (and, indeed, often enhances) the well-being of others. That's why each government should have a set of ground rules to establish its purpose, operating procedures, and—perhaps most important—limitations.

In the United States of America, we set out those rules and limitations in our Constitution. To the extent we have as a nation adhered to that document, we have prospered as a result. The opposite is also true: when we neglect the Constitution, we lose its protections and the benefits that flow from them.

It concerns me greatly that some of our most significant constitutional protections—particularly structural features like federalism and the separation of powers, but also many of the substantive limitations found in the Bill of Rights—have been neglected and weakened over the last eighty years. While it is easy to blame the Supreme Court or certain presidents for this neglect, it is a saving grace of our Republic that the people can remedy the problems created by the Court or the chief executive.

But in order to do that, the people first have to understand the Constitution, and then reinstate it as the centerpiece of American political discourse.

Most Americans are not inclined to willfully disregard the wisdom of our founding documents. Some, however, want to do precisely that; they consider the document quaint, outdated, and an unnecessary impediment to expanding the size, reach, and cost of the federal government.

Accordingly, if we want to preserve, protect, and defend the Constitution—and the many blessings of liberty that come from a government that follows it—the best thing we can do is to keep ourselves (and our fellow citizens) informed about what that document says, how it came into existence, and the nature of the threats facing it. In other words, in the American Republic, knowledge—specifically, a deep and widespread knowledge of the Constitution—is the greatest way to safeguard freedom.

Such knowledge, however, is not transmitted from one generation to another through the bloodstream. It must be taught, learned, and followed in each generation. And whenever that fails to happen, the Constitution—and with it, the liberty and prosperity of the American people—is left unprotected. In my previous book, *Our Lost Constitution,* I quoted an observation by Supreme Court Justice Anthony Kennedy on the importance of understanding the Constitution in order to protect it. Justice Kennedy said: "You cannot preserve what you do not revere; you cannot protect what you have not learned; you cannot defend what you do not know."[1]

Too many Americans today have settled for less than the constitutional, liberty-minded republic they deserve. They have done so not because they don't like the Constitution or need the blessings provided by a government that honors it, but rather because they— like many they have elected to represent them in Washington—have been misinformed (or perhaps, *under*informed) about the kind of government they are entitled to inherit as U.S. citizens.

The good news is that the knowledge that is so crucial to protecting our Constitution has not been entirely lost and can still be recovered with relative ease.

Our system is not "broken"; it is just filled with people who have an incomplete understanding of the brilliant individuals and ideas that established our government some two and a half centuries ago. And unfortunately, it's not just a problem among the people who inhabit Washington, DC. This historical illiteracy is spreading to our schools and our colleges, where it is infecting our kids, who no longer learn about the founding generation with the reverence and awe that, a generation or two ago, was a staple of our public school curricula. They even had a term for it: civic education.

The sad truth is that both of America's major political parties have, to one degree or another, settled into a pattern of undermining the Constitution. Democrats have their own agenda: following a progressive worldview that brings creeping collectivism. But Republicans are also to blame. Time and time again I have watched as my own colleagues in Congress—many of whom I deeply respect—take power away from the people and move it to Washington, and then give it to unelected, unaccountable bureaucrats.

While substantial, our problem is fixable. As Americans continue to see trust in Washington is usually misplaced, they will become more open to the very discussion we need to have—a discussion that will place the Constitution at the center of American political discourse. That will happen naturally as we, as a people, become more familiar with the stories of our founders—those who drafted, ratified, and otherwise influenced the Constitution.

That's why today's America needs Luther Martin. And Mum

Bett. And Canasatego. And Mercy Otis Warren and her brother James. The uncontrolled expansion of the federal government is proof that their voices, and those of other forgotten founders, have been silenced. If they had not been written out of history, their lessons would still be learned today, perhaps preventing us from being hoodwinked by politicians willing to circumvent the Constitution in pursuit of their own political ambitions.

What is most remarkable about the figures in this book is that they are, in many ways, a reflection of the American people—then and now. The figures in this book represent distinct segments of early American society. Some, like James Otis and Mercy Otis Warren, were prosperous residents of urban centers. George Mason came from the landowning aristocracy. Canasatego was descended from the very first Americans, who had inhabited this land for millennia. Mum Bett, later known as Elizabeth Freeman, was viewed as property because of the color of her skin. All of them were human; and like all humans, they had flaws. But each of them saw and fought for something greater and helped to bring a new nation into being. While reading the fascinating stories of these historical figures, I hope you have gained an appreciation not only for the flood of ideas that surged through American society at the time of the Revolution, but also for the individual men and women who developed and disseminated those ideas.

I wrote *Written Out of History* with an eye toward providing readers with more than a simple history lesson. My conscious objective was to create an experience—one that you would find more illuminating and entertaining than can be found in the history books we studied in school. In every chapter I tried to bring to life the sights and sounds and smells of the eighteenth century. I made sure never to knowingly depart from the historical record and my research of these figures. This is because I hoped to offer an intimate look at our national blueprint through the eyes of the individuals who gave it life. I hoped to honor their contributions to the great American story.

Not everyone featured in this book was at the Constitutional Convention in Philadelphia, but a number of those profiled come from the ranks of the Constitution's skeptics—those among the Founding Fathers who, like George Mason and Luther Martin, became known as the Anti-Federalists because of their suspicion of federal power. Many of us are raised to believe that the Constitution was a masterfully crafted document brought into being by a spirited group of reformers who generally saw everything the same way, united in their vision for a democratic republic. But that's not the real story. Or at least that's not the whole story.

Martin, Mason, and others were dissenting voices at the Constitutional Convention. If history eventually proved them right, does that mean the final Constitution got it wrong?

That would indeed be a strange assertion to come from someone who has spent his entire career studying, advocating for, and fighting to protect the principles enshrined in that most important of our founding documents. But in my nearly lifelong study of the Constitution and the era of our nation's founding, I have discovered many stories that challenge what we take to be conventional wisdom about America's birth—the "origin story" of our country. These are the stories of Americans you may never have heard of, and who may not receive much coverage in history books. But all of them, in their own way, helped to explore, test, and refine the concepts of freedom and liberty as they were applied to form what would become the world's greatest republic. Taken together, their threads combine to add richness and depth to the great tapestry of American history.

Aaron Burr's contribution was, in some ways, his downfall—making his story a moving cautionary tale about the excesses of executive power. The leaders of democracies are hardly immune to Lord Acton's observation that "power tends to corrupt and absolute power corrupts absolutely." President Thomas Jefferson, who mercilessly persecuted (and prosecuted) Burr, was no exception. Even a revered founder, who eloquently warned the American people against the dangers of accumulated, unfettered power—and who remained a staunch advocate for keeping power close to the people—fell prey to power's alluring temptation. And Jefferson was hardly the last president to be so tempted.

The barrier between constitutional limited government and tyranny is often a thin one. It was in the first days of the Republic, and it certainly is today. In a system like ours—one that requires citizen participation—it is incumbent upon all of us to recognize and demand virtue and self-restraint in our public servants. The temptations of power are simply too great. Through our collective vigilance over generations, we have largely avoided what so many founding-era Americans feared—that the presidency would turn into a monarchy. Troublingly, however, we have seen incremental movement in that direction from presidents of both political parties. If we are to halt that movement, we must remember the hard lessons of America's third president in his drive to eliminate his political nemesis.

One can draw a direct line from Jefferson's overreach in the Burr case to many other chief executives who, having grown frustrated with a recalcitrant Congress or Supreme Court, have overstepped the Constitution in pursuit of their own ambitions. Examples of this include (but are by no means limited to) Franklin Roosevelt's effort to stack the Supreme Court with those favorable to his New Deal policies; efforts by Lyndon Johnson and Richard Nixon to wiretap political opponents and even their own staff members; and Barack Obama's attempts to circumvent legislative authority through executive orders.

Years before Jefferson put Burr in the dock, Luther Martin was arguing passionately (if perhaps drunkenly) against that very sort of abuse of executive power. That was why Martin was so eager to serve as one of Burr's attorneys, leading him to declare after his victory that he was proud to be among the American lawyers "who cannot be intimidated by fear of presidential vengeance."[2] What would Martin—who so feared a strong executive that he delivered marathon speeches against the idea at the Constitutional Convention before eventually storming out in protest—think today? What would he think of a chief executive who boldly proclaimed his own preference for leading not through the American people's elected representatives in Congress, but through the powers of the executive order, of his own "pen and phone"? Martin could not have imagined the telephone, nor could he have foreseen the development of the Internet and the transformation of the media landscape in ways that allow a presidential administration to shape the news to suit its own political purposes. Yet to this visionary, the threat of an all-powerful executive branch loomed large.

Today, more than 229 years later—after 8 years of a president who continually tested and often overstepped the limits of his constitutional authority, and who has showed us just how far those limits can be pushed in our modern era—Luther Martin looks like quite the sage. It was easy to picture him observing our government in recent years, listening to the latest West Wing press conference by President Obama and murmuring quietly to himself: "A king in everything but name."

Mercy Otis Warren spoke up to make similar arguments against monarchical tendencies in American government, and she was not afraid to direct them at her onetime friend President John Adams. Her fertile pen left much for later generations to gratefully digest. We need more people who aren't afraid to speak up. Good men and women arrive in Washington dreaming of doing good, of changing things for the better. But before long—maybe out of friendship or perhaps a desire to just get along—too many of them fail to speak up and get co-opted by the system.

When Warren warned that "there are no well defined limits of the Judiciary Powers, they seem to be left as a boundless ocean," could she possibly have anticipated how Chief Justice John Roberts would misuse the Supreme Court's judicial power to change the meaning of Obamacare and protect a massive expansion of government? Mercy Otis Warren must live on in the minds of all Americans, particularly those who are concerned about the growth of government and the sneaking supremacy of the executive branch—"the dangerous encroachments of power in too many instances to be named" that she was so prescient to warn against in 1788.

When Warren explained that "the Executive and the Legislative are so dangerously blended as to give just cause of alarm," could she have anticipated just how much Congress—where the people's voice in their government is strongest—has taken a backseat to the presidency over the centuries, to the point where today most of our "laws" in America come not from elected lawmakers but from unelected, unaccountable federal regulators?

When Warren lamented the lack of "anything to prevent the perpetuity of office in the same hands," to keep government officials from developing "the overbearing insolence of office" and remain in touch with "the feelings of the governed," could she have imagined a government staffed with permanent bureaucrats who are almost impossible to dislodge even in the face of failures and scandals? For example, could she have foreseen the seemingly intractable abuse we have seen from the IRS?

Warren's concerns, of course, would only have been heightened by the deterioration of federalism, an idea whose roots in America trace back to the Iroquois Confederacy. Federalism was so eloquently explained by Canasatego that Ben Franklin was moved to print and share the concept, eventually using it as a model for the new American Republic. And while it would ultimately be enshrined in the Constitution's Tenth Amendment and followed faithfully for roughly a century and a half, it was not safe. The twentieth century would claim it as a victim. President Franklin D. Roosevelt, eager to implement his government-expanding New Deal agenda, found that the Tenth Amendment got in his way. He believed that the federal government should have the power to do anything as long as he, FDR, deemed it to be in the best interests of the country. Problems, he thought, "could not be met by merely local action." The states—and therefore the people themselves—would have to be circumvented for the sake of the national interest.

Roosevelt was buoyed by a 1937 Supreme Court decision, *National Labor Relations Board vs. Jones & Laughlin Steel*. In that case, a 5/4 majority opinion written by Chief Justice Charles Evans Hughes declared that under the Constitution's Commerce Clause, even local, intrastate activities are subject to federal control—as long as they have a sufficiently "substantial relation to interstate commerce." The Court clearly sided with the expansive and regulatory goals of the Roosevelt administration—perhaps in response to the implicit threat Roosevelt had made only months earlier to change the Supreme Court nomination procedures and pack the Court with friendly judges.

This decision radically expanded the authority of the Commerce Clause, making it, in effect, the "All Things Affecting Commerce Clause." After 1937, federal authority extended to an almost limitless degree. Federalism, as the United States had known it since its creation, had been effectively eviscerated. The Tenth Amendment had been neutered.

Federalism was one of the two essential structural protections in the Constitution, along with the separation of powers. The two work in tandem to protect individual liberty by preventing any one person or group of people from accumulating too much power. As we have drifted away from federalism, so, too, have we drifted away from the separation of powers. The federal government continues to take power from the people and move it to Washington (undermining federalism), and then within Washington it takes lawmaking power away from the people's elected representatives and gives it to unelected, unaccountable federal bureaucrats (undermining the separation of powers). All of this tends to help the wealthy and well connected, but it does so at the expense of everyone else—especially America's poor and middle class.

The Supreme Court had an opportunity to correct this pattern of constitutional deviation in *NFIB v. Sebelius,* the 2012 case involving Obamacare, in which the Commerce Clause—still enjoying its post-1937 status as a constitutional trump card—was invoked to defend the law's so-called individual mandate, requiring American citizens to purchase health insurance under penalty of law. The Supreme Court—for only the third time in seventy-five years—rejected that argument and concluded that Congress had overstepped its Commerce Clause authority. But then Chief Justice John Roberts did the unthinkable—he decided to rewrite Obamacare in order to save it from the otherwise-inevitable conclusion that it was unconstitutional. As I explain in my 2013 e-book, *Why John Roberts Was Wrong About Healthcare: A Conservative Critique of the Supreme Court's Obamacare Ruling,* he painted what was, in fact, a regulation as a tax, and then deemed it a valid exercise of Congress's authority under the Taxation Clause. In the end, the effect was the same: yet another expansion of federal power went unchecked.

The drift away from federalism and the separation of powers has likewise coincided with a drift away from respect for individual liberties. Elbridge Gerry, who fought to expand protections for the people as the Constitution was being formed, would have been appalled at what I saw in the Senate in the summer of 2014. I stood in shock as several of my colleagues proposed, in all seriousness, an amendment severely limiting the First Amendment. Then Senate Majority Leader Harry Reid and his allies argued that it was time to seriously curtail the First Amendment freedoms of speech and association, which Gerry understood to be so critical to our way of life. The bill's proponents made this argument to make it harder for "outside groups"—in other words, Americans with whom they disagree and (currently) lack the power to control—to pool their resources to raise and spend funds in order to express their various points of view. Members of the press would, of course, be exempted from this regulatory framework, so you'd remain free to express your opinions as long as you owned a newspaper or a broadcasting company. Otherwise, not so much.

Curiously, notwithstanding the First Amendment, public officials in our country have long searched for creative ways to silence dissenters. As we have seen in the unfolding scandal at the Internal Revenue Service, where conservative-oriented organizations were targeted for harassment by the world's most powerful tax collection agency, there is a permanent temptation facing those in power to muzzle dissent.

Yet Elbridge Gerry's legacy has stood in their way of that temptation every time—even if not recognized by name. Thanks to Gerry and others like him, Americans inherited a true national treasure— the Bill of Rights. Gerry was an iconoclast from the start. He defied the New England mold, holding some Anti-Federalist views of the kind more common in the less populous Southern states, which feared they'd be overwhelmed by the desires of New Englanders. The pressure placed on Gerry to sign the Constitution without a bill of rights was undoubtedly enormous, yet he resisted. It takes courage to dissent, especially when there aren't many who share your concerns, and even more so when you stand alone.

Not all of the founding era's victories for individual liberty were struck on battlefields or in stuffy political debates. Elizabeth "Mum Bett" Freeman shook the world from a small Massachusetts courtroom. While she was able to win her own freedom in court by relying on the founding concepts of all being "born free and equal," her case did not, of course, single-handedly end slavery in the United States. Tragically, this barbaric practice lingered on for decades, and its eventual defeat would come at a far greater cost. But Mum Bett—the woman who became Elizabeth Freeman—was ahead of her time. Despite being unable to read or write, she understood the natural rights to which she was entitled and stepped forward to claim them, spurred on by her sense of justice, and forced the courts to do what was just.

That same sense of justice has inspired countless other Americans to step forward through the centuries in an effort to force the courts to do the right thing. When we talk about our commitment to "freedom," we must think about everything that stands in opposition to that idea. Human slavery is the most traumatic and barbarous method by which one person can take away the freedom of another—at times with the assistance of a government willing to authorize and enforce a property right in *another human being*. Does anything that monstrous threaten Americans today? Certainly not. But it remains possible to lose our freedom by degrees, rather than by such sweeping trauma.

Elizabeth "Mum Bett" Freeman showed us that a system that trampled the rights of some Americans—and had been "accepted" for generations—was not only objectively immoral, but utterly at odds with the values of the new nation, whose people recognized their "free and equal" status as human beings. It took decades, and another bloody war, for that idea to fully become the law of the land. It is our responsibility—as the beneficiaries of that struggle—to remain on guard against any erosion of the freedoms we are guaranteed, no matter how small or insignificant they may seem.

We would do well to remember the simple question that Mum Bett asked Theodore Sedgwick as she sought his help with her case: "Won't the law give me my freedom?" The object of any law should be the preservation or expansion of freedom, never its abrogation.

James Otis understood these same basic freedoms and argued for them vociferously against judges installed by King George III. His spirited opposition to out-of-control searches and seizures found its way into the Bill of Rights, in the Fourth Amendment (passed by Congress on September 25, 1789, and ratified by the states on December 15, 1791). The Fourth Amendment affirms the right of the people "to be secure in their persons, houses, papers, and effects, against unreasonable searches and seizures," and declares that "no Warrants shall issue, but upon probable cause, supported by Oath or affirmation, and particularly describing the place to be searched, and the persons or things to be seized."*

The Fourth Amendment remains essential to civil liberties. We may no longer fear red-coated customs officers, but we still confront the dangers of scattershot, overreaching intrusions into our personal data and communications.

---

* Before adoption of the Fourth Amendment in its final form, on June 8, 1789, James Madison offered this proposed amendment language on the subject: "The rights of the people to be secured in their persons, their houses, their papers, and their other property from all unreasonable searches and seizures, shall not be violated by warrants issued without probable cause, supported by oath or affirmation, or not particularly describing the places to be searched, or the persons or things to be seized." (Carol Berkin, *The Bill of Rights: The Fight to Secure America's Liberties* [New York: Simon & Schuster, 2015], 151.)

Times change. Technologies evolve. But basic principles remain the same. In the wake of the terrorist attacks of September 11, 2001, Congress passed the USA PATRIOT Act. The PATRIOT Act, as it has been amended over the years, has been used as a legal justification for government programs collecting data on literally hundreds of millions of Americans, most significantly by monitoring the "metadata"—that is, the details regarding who called whom, when each call occurred, and how long each call lasted—pertaining to the 2.3 trillion minutes of cell phone calls that Americans make each year. The federal government can glean a surprising (and, indeed, disturbing) amount of information about *your* politics, *your* religion, *your* purchasing and travel habits, from the data it collects—all without naming you in any warrant, all without identifying a place to be searched, or even specifying the information the government is seeking.

Luckily, the spirit of James Otis—and his fellow founders—has not yet completely expired. In June 2015, Congress enacted a bill I introduced in the Senate (along with my friend Pat Leahy, a liberal Democrat from Vermont) to address this issue. That bill, the USA FREEDOM ("Uniting and Strengthening America by Fulfilling Rights and Ending Eavesdropping, Dragnet-collection and Online Monitoring") Act, prohibits the bulk collection of records under the PATRIOT Act, the Foreign Intelligence Surveillance Act pen register authority, and national security letter statutes—as well as banning large-scale, indiscriminate data collection, such as all records from an entire state, city, or zip code. The law was enacted on June 2, 2015.

Think about how the government compelled everyone from giant cell phone companies to small-town librarians to assist them in complying with these dragnet orders. Was that very much different from when James Otis protested: "Their menial servants may enter, may break locks, bars, and everything in their way; and whether they break through malice or revenge, no man, no court can inquire. Bare suspicion without oath is sufficient"?[3]

The Bill of Rights that gave us the Fourth Amendment—and the rest of the first ten—was inspired in part by George Mason, who understood the importance of keeping the government out of Americans' private and commercial lives. He may have preferred to stay at home and attend to his business interests, but when his country called, he answered in a big way. He came to epitomize the kind of "citizen-legislator" of which this country is in dire need. Mason did not seek to play politics; rather, he looked out for the interests of his new nation and all of its citizens—even those neglected by much of society. In his fight for a bill of rights, he sought to protect his fellow citizens from a government that tried to grab too much power. In his opposition to the navigation acts, he hoped to unfetter interstate commerce, knowing that doing so would lead to growth and prosperity. And perhaps most tellingly, despite being a slaveholder himself, he stood up to advocate that the United States take the world stage without the stain of slavery upon its conscience.

He was not immediately successful in all of these endeavors, but time has vindicated him. We still struggle with the propensity of the Washington-based bureaucracy to diminish individual freedom, but the Bill of Rights based on Mason's proposals helps keep the problem from getting even worse. Congress still uses the Commerce Clause to justify power grabs like Obamacare, but at least in that instance, the Supreme Court ruled that Congress went too far in relying on the Commerce Clause to require Americans to buy health insurance and penalize those who fail to comply (even if it ultimately upheld that disastrous law on other grounds). And, finally, after a bloody war that started and ended in Mason's native Virginia, slavery was ultimately abolished. That reaffirmed America's commitment to freedom—in every sense of the word—a commitment we must continue to honor every day.

* * *

But more than history, these stories offer warnings and insights for today. As the Age of Obama closes, our constitutional Republic is struggling to rediscover its soul. Indeed, I believe that the stories of Burr and Bett, of the Otises, and of so many others are so important that unless we tell them and reclaim the critical knowledge of these early Americans, our task of restraining government's growth and restoring its checks and balances will become impossible. We will risk a return to the executive power grabs that, over the last eighty years, have loosened our constitutional moorings and set us adrift. Our experiment in limited government will be over and judged a failure.

As dire as that may all sound, what I find encouraging is that these stories offer hope. They provide a model. They provide examples of how real-life (and in some respects ordinary) citizens believed in the power of the individual. They fought for their rights. They foresaw the Leviathan of a federal government trampling their rights. In some cases, their warnings, their pleadings, and their legal arguments went unheeded at the time. In other cases, they succeeded in advancing the cause of freedom, but later faded from history nonetheless. Regardless, if we go back and learn their stories, we can carry on their message today.

The problems stemming from government overreach today are largely due to the fundamental unresolved imbalances that exist between, on the one hand, the federal government and the states (and, therefore, the people who benefit from a system that favors local control in most areas of government); and, on the other hand, between the executive branch and the other two branches of government.

These are precisely the same tensions with which our forgotten founders wrestled. Our first step in joining the battle today over these same issues involves acknowledging our profound debt to those men and women who believed an American Republic would be successful as long as it knew its limits. By channeling voices from the past, I hope this book will inject renewed passion into the debate over what the Constitution means to us today, and on the limits it sets on a power-hungry executive.

America is at a crossroads. The time is coming when the people will need to decide whether to rededicate themselves to our country's founding constitutional principles, or to continue down a path of increased executive power and a permanent redefinition of the American Republic. To truly understand that choice, we must heed the words of our forgotten founders—we must write them back into history.

ACKNOWLEDGMENTS

I am so pleased to have worked once again with Bria Sandford and the excellent team at Sentinel. Matt Latimer, Keith Urbahn, Dylan Colligan, and everyone at Javelin provided great help from the beginning. My wife, Sharon, and our children have given their love and support throughout this project, and for that I will always be grateful. Finally, I would like to recognize the countless Americans who have stood against the encroachment of government throughout our nation's history, and whose stories remain untold in this or any other book. May lovers of liberty everywhere strive to remain worthy of their legacy.

NOTES

INTRODUCTION: THE HAMILTON EFFECT

1. Herbert Croly, *The Promise of American Life* (New York: The Macmillan Company, 1911), 40, 45.
2. *The Federalist Papers,* number 17, Avalon Project, http://avalon.law.yale.edu/18th_century/fed17.asp.
3. Ibid.
4. *The Federalist Papers,* number 32, Avalon Project, http://avalon.law.yale.edu/18th_century/fed32.asp.
5. *The Federalist Papers,* number 45, Avalon Project, http://avalon.law.yale.edu/18th_century/fed45.asp.

CHAPTER 1: AARON BURR AND THE ABUSE OF EXECUTIVE POWER

1. Joseph Whelan, *Jefferson's Vendetta* (New York: Carroll & Graf, 2005), 1–3.
2. Ibid.
3. Virginia Tatnall Peacock, *Famous American Belles of the Nineteenth Century,* 2nd ed. (Philadelphia: J. B. Lippincott Company, 1901), 23.
4. Ibid., 25.
5. Ibid., 22.
6. Alexander Hamilton, National Archives: Founders Online, October 24, 1800, https://founders.archives.gov/documents/Hamilton/01-25-02-0110-0002.
7. John Ferling, "Thomas Jefferson, Aaron Burr and the Election of 1800," Smithsonian.com, November 1, 2004, www.smithsonianmag.com/history/thomas-jefferson-aaron-burr-and-the-election-of-1800-131082359/?no-ist.
8. Ibid.

9. David Harscheid, "Jefferson's Rival (cont'd)," *Washington Post,* February 13, 1993, https://www.washingtonpost.com/archive/opinions/1993/02/13/jeffersons-rival-contd/0d20073f-015e-4fd3-a9b7-f14abcda37e5/?utm_term=.545e1d4b4762.

10. Ferling, "Thomas Jefferson, Aaron Burr and the Election of 1800."

11. Ibid.

12. "The Duel: Alexander Hamilton and Aaron Burr's Duel," *American Experience,* PBS, www.pbs.org/wgbh/amex/duel/index.html; http://www.pbs.org/wgbh/amex/duel/peopleevents/pande17.html.

13. Whelan, *Jefferson's Vendetta,* 77.

14. Sanford Levinson, "Alexander Hamilton Has Relevance in Today's Politics," UT News, May 13, 2016, https://news.utexas.edu/2016/05/13/alexander-hamilton-has-relevance-in-today-s-politics.

15. "Enclosure: Opinions on Aaron Burr," National Archives: Founders Online, https://founders.archives.gov/documents/Hamilton/01-25-02-0156-0002.

16. Ibid.

17. Peacock, *Famous American Belles of the Nineteenth Century,* 20.

18. "The Duel: Alexander Hamilton and Aaron Burr's Duel."

19. Whelan, *Jefferson's Vendetta,* 72.

20. Ibid.

21. "The Least Dangerous but Most Vulnerable Branch: Judicial Independence and the Rights of Citizens," The Pound Institute, 2010, www.poundinstitute.org/sites/default/files/docs/2007PoundForumReport.pdf.

22. "Senate Prepares for Impeachment Trial," United States Senate, www.senate.gov/artandhistory/history/minute/Senate_Tries_Justice.htm.

23. Whelan, *Jefferson's Vendetta,* 74.

24. "Indicted Vice President Bids Senate Farewell," United States Senate, www.senate.gov/artandhistory/history/minute/Indicted_Vice_President_Bids_Senate_Farewell.htm.

25. Whelan, *Jefferson's Vendetta,* 73.

26. "Senate Prepares for Impeachment Trial."

27. Whelan, *Jefferson's Vendetta,* 75.

28. "The Duel: The Burr Conspiracy," *American Experience,* PBS, www.pbs.org/wgbh/amex/duel/index.html; http://www.pbs.org/wgbh/amex/duel/sfeature/burrconspiracy.html.

29. Peter Charles Hoffer, *The Treason Trials of Aaron Burr* (Lawrence: University Press of Kansas), 82–83.

30. Ibid., 81.

31. Thomas Jefferson, "To The Senate and House of Representatives of the United States," The Miller Center, University of Virginia, http://millercenter .org/president/jefferson/speeches/speech-3497.

32. Ibid.

33. Ibid.

34. Ibid.

35. R. Kent Newmyer, "Burr versus Jefferson versus Marshall," *Humanities* 34, no. 3 (May/June 2013), www.neh.gov/humanities/2013/mayjune/feature /burr-versus-jefferson-versus-marshall.

36. "Biographies of the Robes: John Marshall," *The Supreme Court*, PBS, www .pbs.org/wnet/supremecourt/democracy/robes_marshall.html.

37. Ibid.

38. Newmyer, "Burr versus Jefferson versus Marshall."

39. Doug Linder, "The Treason Trial of Aaron Burr," University of Missouri–Kansas City, 2001, http://law2.umkc.edu/faculty/projects/ftrials/burr/bur raccount.html.

40. Newmyer, "Burr versus Jefferson versus Marshall."

41. Joseph Plunkett Brady, *The Trial of Aaron Burr* (New York: The Neale Publishing Company, 1913), 58–59.

42. "To Thomas Jefferson from George Hay, 15 October 1807," National Archives: Founders Online, last modified December 28, 2016, http://founders.archives .gov/documents/Jefferson/99-01-02-6573.

43. Linder, "The Treason Trial of Aaron Burr."

44. Newmyer, "Burr versus Jefferson versus Marshall."

45. "From Thomas Jefferson to James Wilkinson, 20 September 1807," National Archives: Founders Online, last modified December 6, 2016, http://founders .archives.gov/documents/Jefferson/99-01-02-6415.

46. "From Thomas Jefferson to William Thomson, 26 September 1807," National Archives: Founders Online, https://founders.archives.gov/documents/Jeffer son/99-01-02-6452.

CHAPTER 2: LUTHER MARTIN: SOBER ANALYSIS FROM A DRUNK FOUNDER

1. Everett Obrecht, "The Influence of Luther Martin in the Making of the Constitution of the United States," *Maryland Historical Magazine* (September 1932): 183.

2. William Pierce, "Characters in the Convention of the States Held at Philadelphia, May, 1787," Avalon Project, http://avalon.law.yale.edu/18th_century/pierce.asp.

3. Obrecht, "The Influence of Luther Martin in the Making of the Constitution of the United States."

4. "The Founding Fathers: Maryland," National Archives and Records Administration, www.archives.gov/founding-docs/founding-fathers-maryland.

5. "Luther Martin's Letter," January 27, 1788, in Jonathan Elliot, ed., *The Debates in the Several State Conventions on the Adoption of the Federal Constitution as Recommended by the General Convention at Philadelphia, in 1787*, vol. 1 (New York: Burt Franklin, 1888), 349.

6. Luther Martin, *Modern Gratitude, in Five Numbers: Addressed to Richard Raynal Keene, Esq. Concerning a Family Marriage*, 1802, 146–47.

7. Jonathan Elliot, ed., *The Debates in the Several State Conventions on the Adoption of the Federal Constitution as Recommended by the General Convention at Philadelphia in 1787*, vol. 3 (Philadelphia: J. B. Lippincott Company, 1891), 140.

8. Ibid., 140–41.

9. "We the People? or We the States?" Patrick Henry Memorial Foundation, www.redhill.org/speech/we-people-or-we-states.

10. Ibid.

11. Ibid.

12. Luther Martin, "To the Citizens of Maryland," March 18, 1788, in Erastus Scott, ed., *The Federalist and Other Contemporary Papers on the Constitution of the United States* (Baltimore: Scott, Foresman and Company, 1894), 681.

13. Bill Kauffman, *Forgotten Founder, Drunken Prophet: The Life of Luther Martin* (Wilmington, DE: ISI Books, 2008), 22.

14. Frank Moore, ed., *American Eloquence: A Collection of Speeches and Addresses by the Most Eminent Orators of America*, vol. 1 (New York: Appleton, 1880), 382.

15. Quoted in Kauffman, *Forgotten Founder, Drunken Prophet*, 34.

16. "To George Washington from James Madison, 16 April 1787," National Archives: Founders Online, last modified December 28, 2016, http://founders.archives.gov/documents/Washington/04-05-02-0139.

17. Kauffman, *Forgotten Founder, Drunken Prophet*, 34.

18. "Madison Debates, June 27," Avalon Project, http://avalon.law.yale.edu/18th_century/debates_627.asp.

19. "Madison Debates, June 28," Avalon Project, http://avalon.law.yale.edu/18th_century/debates_628.asp.

20. Kauffman, *Forgotten Founder, Drunken Prophet*, 41.

21. Lynne Cheney, *James Madison: A Life Remembered* (New York: Penguin Books, 2014), 135.

22. "Madison Debates, June 28."

23. Kauffman, *Forgotten Founder, Drunken Prophet*, 54.

24. "Notes of the Secret Debates of the Federal Convention of 1787, Taken by the Late Hon Robert Yates, Chief Justice of the State of New York, and One of the Delegates from That State to the Said Convention," Avalon Project, http://avalon.law.yale.edu/18th_century/yates.asp.

25. "Madison Debates, June 28."

26. Kauffman, *Forgotten Founder, Drunken Prophet*, 45.

27. "From George Washington to Alexander Hamilton, 10 July 1787," National Archives: Founders Online, http://founders.archives.gov/documents/Washington/04-05-02-0236.

28. "Madison Debates, July 21," Avalon Project, http://avalon.law.yale.edu/18th_century/debates_721.asp.

29. "Madison Debates, August 17," Avalon Project, http://avalon.law.yale.edu/18th_century/debates_817.asp.

30. "Madison Debates, August 21," Avalon Project, http://avalon.law.yale.edu/18th_century/debates_821.asp.

31. Ibid.

32. Ibid.

33. Ibid.

34. Ibid.

35. Ibid.

36. "Madison Debates, August 22," Avalon Project, http://avalon.law.yale.edu/18th_century/debates_822.asp.

37. Ibid.

38. Ibid.

39. Ibid.

40. Kauffman, *Forgotten Founder, Drunken Prophet*, 61.

41. "Luther Martin's Letter," 350.

42. Ibid., 345.

43. Ibid., 355.

44. Ibid., 349.

45. Ibid., 389.

46. Kauffman, *Forgotten Founder, Drunken Prophet*, 74.

47. "Luther Martin's Letter," 361.

48. Quoted in Kauffman, *Forgotten Founder, Drunken Prophet*, 57.

49. Kauffman, *Forgotten Founder, Drunken Prophet*, 108.

50. Ibid., 117.

51. Ibid., 132.

52. *The Federalist Papers*, number 62, Avalon Project, http://avalon.law.yale .edu/18th_century/fed62.asp.

CHAPTER 3: MERCY OTIS WARREN: THE WOMAN WHO BLOCKED AN AMERICAN KING

1. Alice Brown, *Mercy Warren* (New York: Charles Scribner's Sons, 1896), 93.

2. Ibid., 96.

3. Ibid., 93.

4. Elizabeth Fries Ellet, *The Women of the American Revolution, Volume 1, Part 2* (New York: Charles Scribner, 1856), 79.

5. Morton Bordon, *The Antifederalist Papers* (East Lansing: Michigan State University Press, 1965), 42.

6. Ibid.

7. Jean Fritz, *Cast for a Revolution: Some American Friends and Enemies, 1728–1814* (Boston: Houghton Mifflin Harcourt, 1972), 14; Kate Davies, *Catharine Macaulay and Mercy Otis Warren: The Revolutionary Atlantic and the Politics of Gender* (Oxford: Oxford University Press, 2006), 290.

8. Fritz, *Cast for a Revolution*, 243.

9. "James Warren ('Helvidius Priscus'), December 27, 1787," in Jon L. Wakelyn, *Birth of the Bill of Rights*, vol. 2 (Westport, CT: Greenwood Press, 2004), 112.

10. Nancy Rubin Stuart, *The Muse of the Revolution: The Secret Pen of Mercy Otis Warren and the Founding of a Nation* (Boston: Beacon Press, 2008), 195. The other two were Edmund Randolph and Maryland's Luther Martin.

11. Lance Banning, *The Jeffersonian Persuasion: Evolution of a Party Ideology* (Ithaca, NY: Cornell University Press, 1978), 111.

12. Mercy Otis Warren, *Observations on the New Constitution, and on the Federal and State Conventions: Sic Transit Gloria Americana* (Boston: Richard Seltzer, 1788), www.samizdat.com/warren/observations.html.

13. David O. Stewart, *The Summer of 1787: The Men Who Invented the Constitution* (New York: Simon & Schuster, 2007), 218.

14. Warren, *Observations on the New Constitution*.

15. Ibid.

16. Ibid.

17. Stuart, *The Muse of the Revolution*, 198.

18. Ibid.

19. *The Jury and the Search for Truth: The Case Against Excluding Relevant Evidence*, Hearing Before the Judiciary Committee, United States Senate, 104th Cong., 1st Session, statement by Orrin G. Hatch (Washington, DC: U.S. Government Printing Office, 1995), 151–52.

20. Stuart, *The Muse of the Revolution*, 197.

21. Katherine Anthony, *First Lady of the Revolution: The Life of Mercy Otis Warren* (Port Washington, NY: Kennikat Press, 1958), 214.

22. Stuart, *The Muse of the Revolution*, 246.

23. Ibid., 193. An early biographer of Mercy Warren dismissed *The Sack of Rome* as "long and very dull" (Brown, *Mercy Warren*, 181).

24. Anthony, *First Lady of the Revolution*, 161.

25. *Warren-Adams Letters: Being chiefly a correspondence among John Adams, Samuel Adams, and James Warren* (Boston: Massachusetts Historical Society, 1925), 309; Anthony, *First Lady of the Revolution*, 170; Stuart, *The Muse of the Revolution*, 211, 283.

26. Stewart, *The Summer of 1787*, 220.

27. Ibid., 221.

28. A. J. Langguth, *Patriots: The Men Who Started the American Revolution* (New York: Simon & Schuster, 1988), 551.

29. Stewart, *The Summer of 1787*, 259.

30. "The Electoral Count for the Presidential Election of 1789," Internet Archive: The Papers of George Washington, November 12, 2016, https://web.archive.org/web/20130914141726/http://gwpapers.virginia.edu/documents/presidential/electoral.html.

31. Mercy Warren, *History of the Rise, Progress and Termination of the American Revolution, interspersed with Biographical, Political and Moral Observations, Volume III* (Boston: E. Larkin, 1805), 304; Ray Raphael, *Founders: The People Who Brought You a Nation* (New York: The New Press, 2009), 497; Larry E. Tise, *The American Counterrevolution: A Retreat from Liberty, 1783–1800* (Mechanicsburg, PA: Stackpole Books, 1998), 495.

32. Warren, *History of the Rise, Progress and Termination of the American Revolution*, 392; Anthony, *First Lady of the Revolution*, 218.

33. Warren, *History of the Rise, Progress and Termination of the American Revolution*, 394.

34. Ibid., 395.

35. *Correspondence between John Adams and Mercy Warren Relating to Her "History*

of the American Revolution," July–August, 1807 (Boston: Massachusetts Historical Society, 1878), 422.

36. Ibid., 490–91; Anthony, *First Lady of the Revolution*, 215.

37. Stuart, *The Muse of the Revolution*, 256.

38. *Correspondence between John Adams and Mercy Warren Relating to Her "History of the American Revolution,"* 328; Anthony, *First Lady of the Revolution*, 215.

39. *Correspondence between John Adams and Mercy Warren Relating to Her "History of the American Revolution,"* 489; Jeffrey H. Richards, *Mercy Otis Warren* (New York: Twayne Publishers, 1995), 147.

40. *Correspondence between John Adams and Mercy Warren Relating to Her "History of the American Revolution,"* 463; Anthony, *First Lady of the Revolution*, 215.

41. *Correspondence between John Adams and Mercy Warren Relating to Her "History of the American Revolution,"* 463; Anthony, *First Lady of the Revolution*, 216.

42. *Correspondence between John Adams and Mercy Warren Relating to Her "History of the American Revolution,"* 489; Richards, *Mercy Otis Warren*, 147.

43. Rosemarie Zaggari, *A Woman's Dilemma: Mercy Otis Warren and the American Revolution* (Wheeling, IL: Harlan Davidson, 1995), 142.

44. Anthony, *First Lady of the Revolution*, 162–63.

45. "Mercy Otis Warren," National History Day, Massachusetts Historical Society, www.masshist.org/education/nhdexamples/mow.

46. "The Tradition of Anglo-American Mourning Jewelry: Jewelry Containing Hair," Massachusetts Historical Society, www.masshist.org/features /mourning-jewelry/containing-hair.

CHAPTER 4: JOIN OR DIE: CANASATEGO, BEN FRANKLIN, AND THE CONFEDERACY IN THE WILDERNESS

1. This quotation is based on Franklin's account, published in Carl Van Doren and Julian P. Boyd, eds., *Indian Treaties Printed by Benjamin Franklin* (Philadelphia: Historical Society of Pennsylvania, 1938).

2. "From Benjamin Franklin to James Parker, 20 March 1751," National Archives: Founders Online, last modified December 28, 2016, http://founders.archives .gov/documents/Franklin/01-04-02-0037.

3. "The Constitution of the Iroquois Nations," in *Native Americans and Political Participation: A Reference Handbook* (Santa Barbara, CA: ABC-CLIO, 2005), 202.

4. Bruce E. Johansen, "Forgotten Founders: The Pre-Columbian Republic," Ipswich, Massachusetts, www.tnellen.com/cybereng/FF/FF.html#TOC.

5. Ibid.

6. Ibid.

7. Walter Isaacson, *Benjamin Franklin: An American Life* (New York: Simon & Schuster, 2003), 37.

8. "William Penn to the Kings of the Indians in Pennsylvania, October 18, 1681," Historical Society of Pennsylvania, http://digitalhistory.hsp.org /pafrm/doc/william-penn-kings-indians-pennsylvania-october-18-1681.

9. William Sawyer, "The Six Nations Confederacy During the American Revolution," Fort Stanwix National Monument, National Park Service, www .nps.gov/fost/learn/historyculture/the-six-nations-confederacy-during-the -american-revolution.htm#CP_JUMP_3550115.

10. Bruce E. Johansen, "Forgotten Founders: Our Indians Have Outdone the Romans," Ipswich, Massachusetts, www.tnellen.com/cybereng/FF/FF.htm l#TOC.

11. Bruce E. Johansen, "Forgotten Founders: Such an Union," Ipswich, Massachusetts, www.tnellen.com/cybereng/FF/FF.html#TOC.

12. Ibid.

13. Johansen, "Forgotten Founders."

14. Quoted in ibid.

15. Ibid. These quotations are paraphrased from an account, not exact.

16. Isaacson, *Benjamin Franklin*, 159.

17. Johansen, "Forgotten Founders."

18. Quoted in Isaacson, *Benjamin Franklin*, 157.

19. Ibid., 159.

20. Quoted in Daniel Richter, *Friends and Enemies in Penn's Woods: Colonists, Indians, and the Racial Construction of Pennsylvania* (University Park, PA: Penn State University Press, 2010).

21. Isaacson, *Benjamin Franklin*, 160.

22. Ibid., 161.

23. Van Doren and Boyd, eds., *Indian Treaties Printed by Benjamin Franklin, 1736–1762*, 78.

24. "This Week in History—July 14–20, 1775: Benjamin Franklin Submits His Articles of Confederation and Perpetual Union," The Schiller Institute, July 2013, http://schillerinstitute.org/educ/hist/eiw_this_week/v5n29_jul14 _1775.html.

25. "Journals of the Continental Congress—Franklin's Articles of Confederation;

July 21, 1775," Avalon Project, http://avalon.law.yale.edu/18th_century
/contcong_07-21-75.asp.

26. Quoted in Vine Deloria and Raymond J. DeMallie, eds., *Documents of American Indian Diplomacy: Treaties, Agreements, and Conventions, 1775–1979*, vol. 1 (Norman: University of Oklahoma Press, 1999), 35.

27. Quoted in Ibid.

28. Ibid.

29. Ibid.

30. Quoted in "Iroquois (Haudenosaunee) Confederacy," in *The Encyclopedia of Native American Legal Tradition*, Bruce Johansen, ed. (Westport, CT: Greenwood Press, 1998), 157.

31. "Journals of the Continental Congress."

32. "The Articles of Confederation, 1777," The Gilder Lehrman Institute of American History, www.gilderlehrman.org/history-by-era/war-for
-independence/resources/articles-confederation-1777.

33. *The Federalist Papers,* number 45, Avalon Project, http://avalon.law.yale
.edu/18th_century/fed45.asp.

CHAPTER 5: THE BILL OF RIGHTS: ELBRIDGE GERRY'S "DANGEROUS" IDEA

1. "Declaration of Independence, July 4, 1776," Avalon Project, http://avalon
.law.yale.edu/18th_century/declare.asp.

2. Though the scene is imagined, the quotation is documented in John Ferling's *John Adams: A Life* (Knoxville: University of Tennessee Press, 1992), 345.

3. Ibid.

4. George Athan Billias, *Elbridge Gerry: Founding Father and Republican Statesman* (New York: McGraw-Hill, 1976), 7.

5. Elbridge Gerry to Ann Gerry (May 30, 1787), Constitutional Sources Project, www.consource.org/document/elbridge-gerry-to-ann-gerry-1787-5-30.

6. Ibid.

7. M. E. Bradford, *Founding Fathers: Brief Lives of the Framers of the United States Constitution,* 2nd ed. (Lawrence: University Press of Kansas, 1994), 6.

8. Samuel Eliot Morrison, *By Land and by Sea* (New York: Alfred A. Knopf, 1953), 186.

9. Ibid., 198.

10. "Subjects for Master's Degree," *Harvard Crimson,* March 26, 1884, www
.thecrimson.com/article/1884/3/26/subjects-for-masters-degree-we-have.

11. Billias, *Elbridge Gerry,* 86.

12. James T. Austin, *The Life of Elbridge Gerry*, vol. 1 (Boston: Wells & Lilly, 1828), 324.

13. Billias, *Elbridge Gerry*, 175.

14. Ibid., 142.

15. Quoted in Mark O. Hatfield, "Vice Presidents of the United States" (Washington, DC: U.S. Government Printing Office, 1997), 63–68, www.senate.gov/artandhistory/history/resources/pdf/elbridge_gerry.pdf.

16. "Madison Debates, May 29," Avalon Project, http://avalon.law.yale.edu/18th_century/debates_529.asp.

17. Greg Bradsher, "A Founding Father in Dissent," *Prologue* 38, no. 2 (Summer 2006), National Archives, www.archives.gov/publications/prologue/2006/spring/gerry.html.

18. "Report of Proceedings in Congress; February 21, 1787," Avalon Project, http://avalon.law.yale.edu/18th_century/const04.asp.

19. Bradsher, "A Founding Father in Dissent."

20. Ibid.

21. "Madison Debates, June 29," Avalon Project, http://avalon.law.yale.edu/18th_century/debates_629.asp.

22. Quoted in "Rest and Recuperation," Independence National Historical Park, National Park Service, www.nps.gov/inde/learn/historyculture/rest-and-recuperation.htm.

23. Bradsher, "A Founding Father in Dissent."

24. *The Federalist Papers*, number 63, Avalon Project, http://avalon.law.yale.edu/18th_century/fed63.asp.

25. Richard Beeman, *Plain, Honest Men: The Making of the American Constitution* (New York: Random House, 2009), 155.

26. Bradsher, "A Founding Father in Dissent."

27. Ibid.

28. Ibid.

29. Ibid.

30. "Madison Debates, September 5," Avalon Project, http://avalon.law.yale.edu/18th_century/debates_905.asp.

31. "Madison Debates, September 9," Avalon Project, http://avalon.law.yale.edu/18th_century/debates_907.asp.

32. Billias, *Elbridge Gerry*, 176.

33. *The Federalist Papers*, number 84, Avalon Project, http://avalon.law.yale.edu/18th_century/fed84.asp.

34. Ibid.

35. Ibid.

36. "Madison Debates, September 12," Avalon Project, http://avalon.law.yale
.edu/18th_century/debates_912.asp.

37. Elbridge Gerry to the Massachusetts state legislature, in Jonathan Elliot's
*The Debates in the Several State Conventions on the Adoption of the Federal Con-
stitution,* http://memory.loc.gov/cgi-bin/query/r?ammem/hlaw:@field(DO
CID+@lit(ed001220)).

38. Ibid.

39. Ibid.

40. Ibid.

41. Billias, *Elbridge Gerry,* 229.

42. Ibid.

43. Ibid., 231.

44. Some liberals today attempt to argue that the Second Amendment applies
only to state militias, but that view is supported neither by the text nor by
the context of Congress's deliberation. For more, see Nelson Lund's "The
Second Amendment and the Inalienable Right to Self-Defense" (Heritage
Foundation, April 2014), www.heritage.org/research/reports/2014/04/the
-second-amendment-and-the-inalienable-right-to-self-defense.

45. Billias, *Elbridge Gerry,* 232.

46. "To John Adams from Rufus King, 23 November 1814," National Archives:
Founders Online, last modified December 28, 2016, http://founders.archives
.gov/documents/Adams/99-02-02-6352.

47. Ibid.

CHAPTER 6: MUM BETT: THE SLAVE WHO CLAIMED HER RIGHTS

1. American history has been tragically robbed of a full, thorough, and
completely authenticated account of the life of Mum Bett, later known as
Elizabeth Freeman. Besides the scant court record—written in opaque
eighteenth-century legal jargon—most of the accounts of her life and
her trial were written after the fact. Some of the writers were closer to Bett
than others, but nevertheless many of the accounts are incomplete or even
contradictory—and there remain holes in the story that have been filled in
over the years with speculation. The account here is the result of diligent
consultation of many of the available sources and should be taken as a faithful synthesis of such aspects of the information found therein as would

compose a solid narrative. In some instances, details or dialogue have been imagined for the sake of the narrative or as an attempt to present a complete record, but these instances should remain faithful to the story and spirit of Mum Bett's life.

2. Catherine Maria Sedgwick, "Slavery in New England," *Bentley's Miscellany* 34 (1853): 419.

3. The Trustees of Reservations, *The Ashley House Management Plan, 2007*, page 3-2, www.thetrustees.org/assets/documents/places-to-visit/managementplans /B_AshleyHouse_MP2007.pdf.

4. Ibid., page 3-8.

5. Jon Swan, "The Slave Who Sued for Freedom," *American Heritage* (March 1990): 51.

6. Robert J. Taylor, *Western Massachusetts in the Revolution* (Providence, RI: Brown University Press, 1954), 82.

7. Sedgwick, "Slavery in New England," 421.

8. Ibid.

9. Ibid.

10. Quoted in ibid., 419.

11. Ibid., 421.

12. Ibid., 418.

13. The Trustees of Reservations, *The Ashley House Management Plan, 2007*, page 3-9.

14. Sedgwick, "Slavery in New England," 418.

15. "Sheffield Declaration (1773)," Constitution Society, www.constitution .org/bcp/sheffield_declaration.html.

16. Ibid.

17. Ibid.

18. Ibid.

19. Lillian E. Preiss, *Sheffield, Frontier Town* (Sheffield, MA: Sheffield Bicentennial Committee, 1976), 40.

20. Ibid., 44.

21. Ibid., 42.

22. Ibid.

23. "The Massachusetts Constitution of 1780," Massachusetts Court System, www.mass.gov/courts/court-info/sjc/edu-res-center/jn-adams/the -massachusetts-constitution-of-1780.html.

24. Sedgwick, "Slavery in New England," 418.

25. Henry Dwight Sedgwick, "The Practicability of the Abolition of Slavery," quoted in *The United States Magazine and Democratic Review* 7 (1840): 131.

26. Swan, "The Slave Who Sued for Freedom," 52.

27. Harriet Martineau, *Retrospect of Western Travel in Three Vols*, vol. 1 (London: Saunders and Otley, 1838), 246.

28. Sedgwick, "Slavery in New England," 421.

29. Martineau, *Retrospect of Western Travel in Three Vols*, vol. 1, 246.

30. Charles Taylor, *History of Great Barrington (Berkshire County), Massachusetts* (Great Barrington, MA: Clark W. Bryan & Co., 1882), 288.

31. "Elizabeth Freeman: Fighting for Freedom," The Trustees of Reservations, February 2012, www.thetrustees.org/what-we-care-about/history-culture /elizabeth-freeman-fighting-for-freedom.html?referrer=https://www.goo gle.com.

32. Arthur Zilversmit, "Quok Walker, Mumbet and the Abolition of Slavery in Massachusetts," in *Abolitionism and American Law*, ed. John R. McKivigan (New York: Garland Publishing, Inc., 1999), 59.

33. "A History of the Litchfield Law School," Litchfield Historical Society, www.litchfieldhistoricalsociety.org/history/law_school.php.

34. Zilversmit, "Quok Walker, Mumbet and the Abolition of Slavery in Massachusetts," 60.

35. *Brom & Bett v. J. Ashley Esq.*, court record, http://mumbet.com/index.php /77-articles/mumbet/50-court.

36. Ibid.

37. Ibid.

38. Zilversmit, "Quok Walker, Mumbet and the Abolition of Slavery in Massachusetts," 64.

39. Clarence Fanto, "County History Goes National Tonight," *The Berkshire Eagle*, April 8, 2012, www.berkshireeagle.com/stories/county-history-goes-national -tonight,431605.

40. *Brom & Bett v. J. Ashley Esq.*, court record.

41. Ibid.

42. Ibid.

43. François-Alexandre-Frédéric duc de La Rochefoucauld-Liancourt, *Travels Through the United States of North America*, vol. 3 (London: R. Phillips, 1800), 326.

44. Sedgwick, "The Practicability of the Abolition of Slavery," 40.

45. Zilversmit, "Quok Walker, Mumbet and the Abolition of Slavery in Massachusetts," 61.

46. Lolly Bowean, "Arthur Zilversmit, 1932–2005," *Chicago Tribune*, September 5, 2005, http://articles.chicagotribune.com/2005-09-05/news/0509050030 _1_history-nazi-invasion-new-york.

47. *Brom & Bett v. J. Ashley Esq.*, court record.

48. Ibid.

49. Zilversmit, "Quok Walker, Mumbet and the Abolition of Slavery in Massachusetts," 61.

50. Ibid.

51. Ibid.

52. Martineau, *Retrospect of Western Travel in Three Vols,* vol. 1, 246.

53. Swan, "The Slave Who Sued for Freedom," 55.

54. Sedgwick, "The Practicability of the Abolition of Slavery," 40.

55. Ibid.

56. Laurie Robertson-Lorant, "Mumbet: Truth Was Her Nature," *Special Places,* The Trustees of Reservations, Summer 2006, www.thetrustees.org/what-we -care-about/history-culture/mumbet-truth-was-her-nature.html.

57. Swan, "The Slave Who Sued for Freedom," 55.

58. Mary E. Dewey, ed., *Life and Letters of Catherine Maria Sedgwick* (New York: Harper & Brothers), 41–42.

59. "Boston African American National Historic Site," National Park Service, www.nps.gov/nr/travel/cultural_diversity/Boston_African_American _National_Historic_Site.html.

CHAPTER 7: JAMES OTIS AND THE TRIAL THAT GAVE US THE FOURTH AMENDMENT

1. M. H. Smith, *The Writs of Assistance Case* (Berkeley: University of California Press, 1978), 116.

2. Ibid., 140, 504; Harlow Giles Unger, *American Tempest: How the Boston Tea Party Sparked a Revolution* (Cambridge, MA: Da Capo Press, 2011), 36.

3. Jean Fritz, *Cast for a Revolution: Some American Friends and Enemies, 1728–1814* (Boston: Houghton Mifflin Harcourt, 1972), 34; Hiller B. Zobel, *The Boston Massacre* (New York: W. W. Norton, 1970), 14; Smith, *The Writs of Assistance Case,* 130, 506. Word of King George II's death did not reach Boston until December 27 (Zobel, *The Boston Massacre,* 14; Smith, *The Writs of Assistance Case,* 130; Lawrence Henry Gipson, "Aspects of the Beginning of the American Revolution in Massachusetts Bay 1760–1762," *Proceedings of the American Antiquarian Association* [April 1957]: 21).

4. James Otis, *The rudiments of Latin prosody: with, A dissertation on letters, and the*

principles of harmony, in poetic and prosaic composition (Boston: Benj. Mecam, 1760), passim.

5. Francis Bowen, *The Life of James Otis* (Boston: Charles C. Little and James Brown, 1844), 24; *Encyclopedia Americana*, vol. 9 (Philadelphia: Thomas Cowperthwait & Co., 1841), 453.

6. Reverend H. Hewitt, "James Otis, Jr.," *New England Magazine*, April 1886, 320; Ray Raphael, *Founders: The People Who Brought You a Nation* (New York: The New Press, 2009), 15; Nancy Rubin Stuart, *The Muse of the Revolution: The Secret Pen of Mercy Otis Warren and the Founding of a Nation* (Boston: Beacon Press, 2008), 16.

7. Charles Francis Adams, ed., *The Works of John Adams, Second President of the United States, Volume II* (Boston: Charles C. Little and James Brown, 1850), 47fn.

8. Harlow Giles Unger, *American Tempest: How the Boston Tea Party Sparked a Revolution* (Cambridge, MA: Da Capo Press, 2011), 38.

9. Ibid.

10. Lawrence Henry Gipson, "Aspects of the Beginning of the American Revolution in Massachusetts Bay 1760–1762," *Proceedings of the American Antiquarian Association* (April 1957): 21; Jean Fritz, *Cast for a Revolution: Some American Friends and Enemies, 1728–1814* (Boston: Houghton Mifflin Harcourt, 1972), 31–32.

11. Thomas P. Slaughter, *Independence: The Tangled Roots of the American Revolution* (New York: Hill & Wang, 2014), 150; Gipson, "Aspects of the Beginning of the American Revolution," 22.

12. Fritz, *Cast for a Revolution*, 34; Stuart, *The Muse of the Revolution*, 25.

13. Smith, *The Writs of Assistance Case*, 138.

14. Zobel, *The Boston Massacre*, 14; Slaughter, *Independence*, 149; Smith, *The Writs of Assistance Case*, 131; Benjamin L. Carp, *Defiance of the Patriots: The Boston Tea Party and the Making of America* (New Haven, CT: Yale University Press), 34.

15. Adams, ed., *The Works of John Adams*, 124fn.

16. William Tudor, *The Life of James Otis of Massachusetts* (Boston: Wells & Lilly, 1840), 57; Adams, ed., *The Works of John Adams*, 247; James K. Hosmer, *The Life of Thomas Hutchinson, Royal Governor of the Province of Massachusetts Bay* (Boston: Houghton, Mifflin and Company, 1896), 53; John Adams, *James Otis, Samuel Adams, and John Hancock: Tributes to These as the Three Principal Movers and Agents of the American Revolution* (Boston: Old South Leaflets,

1907), 60. John Adams estimated that Otis Jr.'s resigned advocate generalship was "worth twice" the two-hundred-pound chief justiceship salary that his father had forfeited to Hutchinson: "The son must have been a most dutiful and affectionate son to the father" (*Novanglus, and Massachusetts; or, Political Essays* . . . [Boston: Hews & Goss, 1819], 243).

17. Hosmer, *The Life of Thomas Hutchinson, Royal Governor of the Province of Massachusetts Bay,* 49; Fritz, *Cast for a Revolution,* 34; Stuart, *The Muse of the Revolution,* 24; Raphael, *Founders,* 16.

18. Alice Brown, *Mercy Warren* (New York: Charles Scribner's Sons, 1896), 40.

19. Tudor, *The Life of James Otis of Massachusetts,* 60. These are John Adams's words.

20. Fritz, *Cast for a Revolution,* 44.

21. Brown, *Mercy Warren,* 43; Smith, *The Writs of Assistance Case,* 267.

22. Smith, *The Writs of Assistance Case,* 270.

23. *The Granite Monthly: A New Hampshire Magazine* 39 (October 1907): 342; Zobel, *The Boston Massacre,* 14.

24. Smith, *The Writs of Assistance Case,* 281.

25. Mark G. Spencer, *The Bloomsbury Encyclopedia of the American Enlightenment, Volume 2* (New York: Bloomsbury, 2015), 1026.

26. Edward Channing, *A History of the United States: The American Revolution, 1761–1789* (New York: The Macmillan Company, 1912), 4.

27. Adams, ed., *The Works of John Adams, Second President of the United States, Volume X,* 247; Spencer, *The Bloomsbury Encyclopedia of the American Enlightenment, Volume 2,* 1027.

28. Tudor, *The Life of James Otis of Massachusetts,* 88–89; Albert Bushnell Hart and Edward Channin, eds., *James Otis's Speech on Writs of Assistance 1761* (New York: Parker P. Simmons, 1906), 29.

29. Hewitt, "James Otis, Jr.," 322; Hart and Channin, eds., *James Otis's Speech on Writs of Assistance 1761,* 23; Stuart, *The Muse of the Revolution,* 25.

30. Hart and Channin, eds., *James Otis's Speech on Writs of Assistance 1761,* 5; Gipson, "Aspects of the Beginning of the American Revolution in Massachusetts Bay 1760–1762," 26; *The New England Quarterly* 79, no. 4 (December 2006): 536.

31. Bowen, *The Life of James Otis,* 55; Claude H. Van Tyne, *The Causes of the War of Independence* (Boston: Houghton, Mifflin Company, 1922), 133.

32. Adams, ed., *The Works of John Adams, Second President of the United States, Volume X,* 183; *The New England Quarterly* 79, no. 4 (December 2006): 541.

33. Tudor, *The Life of James Otis of Massachusetts*, 66–67.

34. Adams, ed., *The Works of John Adams, Second President of the United States, Volume X*, 247; Hosmer, *The Life of Thomas Hutchinson, Royal Governor of the Province of Massachusetts Bay*, 58; George Elliot Howard, *Preliminaries of the Revolution, 1763–1775*, vol. 8 (New York: Harper & Brothers, 1905), 76; Stuart, *The Muse of the Revolution*, 25; Raphael, *Founders*, 15.

35. John Adams, *James Otis, Samuel Adams, and John Hancock*, 60.

36. Smith, *The Writs of Assistance Case*, 411–12; Andrew Stephen Walmsley, *Thomas Hutchinson and the Origins of the American Revolution* (New York: New York University Press, 1999), 44–45.

37. Smith, *The Writs of Assistance Case*, 413fn; Walmsley, *Thomas Hutchinson and the Origins of the American Revolution*, 45; Gipson, "Aspects of the Beginning of the American Revolution in Massachusetts Bay 1760–1762," 30.

38. Adams, ed., *The Works of John Adams, Second President of the United States, Volume X*, 248; Van Tyne, *The Causes of the War of Independence*, 178; John W. Johnson, *Historic U.S. Court Cases: An Encyclopedia* (New York: Routledge, 2001), 28; Slaughter, *Independence*, 150; Raphael, *Founders*, 13; *The New England Quarterly* 79, no. 4 (December 2006): 536.

39. *The Bostonian* (April 1895), 24.

40. James Otis, *The Rights of the British Colonies Asserted and Proved* (Boston & London: J. Almon, 1764), 43; http://oll.libertyfund.org/titles/2335.

41. Tudor, *The Life of James Otis of Massachusetts*, 361–62.

42. Jacob Abbott, *American History*, vol. 5 (New York: Thomas Y. Crowell & Co., 1863), 140.

43. *The London Chronicle*, November 4, 1769; http://www.rarenewspapers.com /view/601343.

44. Abbott, *American History*, 140.

45. *Massachusetts Gazette*, September 11, 1769; http://www.rarenewspapers.com /view/601343.

46. Ibid.

47. Stuart, *The Muse of the Revolution*, 40.

48. Tudor, *The Life of James Otis of Massachusetts*, 474–75.

49. "[January 1770]," National Archives: Founders Online, last modified October 5, 2016, http://founders.archives.gov/documents/Adams/01-01-02-0014 -0001. [Original source: *The Adams Papers*, Diary and Autobiography of John Adams, vol. 1, 1755–1770, ed. L. H. Butterfield (Cambridge, MA: Harvard University Press, 1961), 348–49].

50. Tudor, *The Life of James Otis of Massachusetts*, 475.

51. Benjamin Franklin Perry, *Biographical Sketches of Eminent American States-men, with Speeches, Addresses and Letters* (Philadelphia: Ferree Press, 1887), 246.

CHAPTER 8: GEORGE MASON: DEFENDER OF INDIVIDUAL AND ECONOMIC FREEDOM

1. Dumas Malone, Hirst Milhollen, and Milton Kaplan, *The Story of the Dec-laration of Independence* (Oxford: Oxford University Press, 1975), 19.

2. Jeff Broadwater, *George Mason, Forgotten Founder* (Chapel Hill: University of North Carolina Press, 2009), 24.

3. Jeff Broadwater, "George Mason (1725–1792)," *Encyclopedia Virginia*, Virginia Foundation for the Humanities (March 6, 2014), http://www.ency clopediavirginia.org/Mason_George_1725-1792.

4. "Virginia Nonimportation Resolutions, 17 May 1769," *The Papers of Thomas Jefferson*, ed. Julian P. Boyd, vol. 1, 1760–1776 (Princeton, NJ: Princeton University Press, 1950), 27–31.

5. "To Thomas Jefferson from Edmund Pendleton, 24 May 1776," National Archives: Founders Online, last modified December 28, 2016, http://found ers.archives.gov/documents/Jefferson/01-01-02-0157.

6. Broadwater, *George Mason, Forgotten Founder*, 88.

7. Ibid., 89.

8. "George Mason to Virginia Delegates, 3 and 20 April 1781," National Archives: Founders Online, last modified December 28, 2016, http://found ers.archives.gov/documents/Madison/01-03-02-0023.

9. Broadwater, *George Mason, Forgotten Founder*, 74.

10. Ibid., 157.

11. Ibid., 161.

12. "Madison Debates, September 15," Avalon Project, http://avalon.law.yale .edu/18th_century/debates_915.asp.

13. Quoted in Jonathan Elliot, ed., *The Debates in the Several State Conven-tions on the Adoption of the Federal Constitution as Recommended by the General Convention at Philadelphia, in 1787*, vol. 3 (Philadelphia: J. B. Lippincott Company, 1891), 604.

14. "Madison Debates, August 22," Avalon Project, http://avalon.law.yale.edu /18th_century/debates_822.asp.

15. Broadwater, *George Mason, Forgotten Founder*, 192.

16. Helen Hill Miller, *George Mason, Gentleman Revolutionary* (Chapel Hill: University of North Carolina Press, 1975), 261.

17. Ibid., 262.

18. "Madison Debates, September 12," Avalon Project, http://avalon.law.yale.edu/18th_century/debates_912.asp.

19. Bill Kauffman, *Forgotten Founder, Drunken Prophet: The Life of Luther Martin* (Wilmington, DE: ISI Books, 2008), 65.

20. "From James Madison to Thomas Jefferson, 24 October 1787," National Archives: Founders Online, last modified December 28, 2016, http://founders.archives.gov/documents/Madison/01-10-02-0151.

21. "George Mason's Objections to the Constitution," Gunston Hall, http://www.gunstonhall.org/library/archives/manuscripts/objections.html.

22. Ibid.

23. Ibid.

24. Quoted in Kate Mason Rowland, *The Life of George Mason, 1725–1792* (New York: G.P. Putnam's Sons, 1892), 163.

25. Ibid.

26. Broadwater, *George Mason, Forgotten Founder*, 242.

27. "Gunston Hall," Frommer's, http://www.frommers.com/destinations/mount-vernon/attractions/213140.

28. Gretchen McKay, "George Mason's Gunston Hall Plantation Offers a Look at 18-Century Virginia Life," *Pittsburgh Post-Gazette*, April 10, 2016, http://www.post-gazette.com/life/travel/2016/04/10/George-Mason-s-Gunston-Hall-plantation-offers-a-look-at-18-century-Virginia-life/stories/201604100031.

CONCLUSION: WRITING OUR FORGOTTEN FOUNDERS BACK INTO HISTORY

1. U.S. Supreme Court justice Anthony Kennedy, "Text of Justice Kennedy's 2009 Commencement Address," *Stanford Report*, June 14, 2009, http://news.stanford.edu/news/2009/june17/kennedy_text061709.html.

2. Michael Ariens, *Lost and Found: David Hoffman and the History of American Legal Ethics*, 571 Ark.L.Rev. 67 (2014) http://media.law.uark.edu/arklawreview/2015/02/23/lost-and-found-david-hoffman-and-the-history-of-american-legal-ethics/#_ftn63.

3. William Tudor, *The Life of James Otis of Massachusetts* (Boston: Wells & Lilly, 1840), 66–67.

INDEX

Don't miss Senator Mike Lee's previous book on the forgotten origins of our founding document.

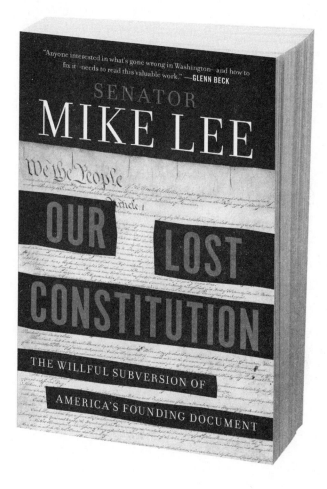

"Anyone interested in what's gone wrong in Washington—and how to fix it—needs to read this valuable work." —**GLENN BECK**

SENATOR
MIKE LEE

We the People

Article 1

OUR LOST CONSTITUTION

THE WILLFUL SUBVERSION OF
AMERICA'S FOUNDING DOCUMENT

"Defenders of the Constitution, this is a must-read book for you."
—**Mark Levin**